FROM HERO TO SERVANT TO MYSTIC

D0840089

From Hero to Servant to Mystic

Navigating the Deeper Waters of Priestly Spirituality

Scott P. Detisch

LITURGICAL PRESS
Collegeville, Minnesota

www.litpress.org

Contents

Acknowledgments

My own spiritual journey as a priest began with the inspiration I received from the incredible models of authentic and fulfilling priesthood I encountered before and after ordination, especially in my home diocese of Erie, Pennsylvania. I have watched these priests with admiration; I have been taught and mentored by them, ministered alongside them, prayed with them, and enjoyed friendships with many of them. These priests have been amazing heroes, dedicated servants, and powerful mystics in the church and in my life. To all of them I offer this "spiritual biography" of priesthood as an act of thanksgiving. They are the ones who initially and continually helped me "put out into the deep water" and cultivated in me a desire to be a good pastoral minister for God's People.

The recognition that being an effective pastoral minister has to be paired with being a deeply spiritual person was firmly implanted in me through the initial priestly formation, theological education, and pastoral training I received at Christ the King Seminary in East Aurora, New York. The Franciscans of the Holy Name Province who oversaw the seminary at that time, the priests of the Diocese of Buffalo who helped to staff it, the religious women and laypersons who were key members of the faculty all had a deep and lasting impression on my continued development as a human being and on my continued formation as a priest. I am equally grateful to the amazing spiritual directors, mentors, and retreat directors who have guided me in keeping priestly ministry tethered to the inner life, especially Sr. Joan Wagner, SSJ, Fr. Peter Drilling, Fr. Rick Reina, Fr. Daniel McLellan, OFM, Sr. Maria McCoy, CSJ, and Fr. Jerome Simmons. These wise persons taught me how to pray, how to ponder, and how to hold the vicissitudes of life in redemptive contact with the Indwelling of God. My hope is that what I offer in this book is a fitting reflection of the deep wisdom and spiritual insight that each of them shared with me.

The motivation to write this book has come not only from my own struggles to grow in the spiritual life and priestly ministry, when I had to surrender (sometimes painfully) into a whole new level of archetypal energy, but also from my years as a faculty member in priestly formation work. I am indebted to the colleagues with whom I served at Christ the King Seminary (East Aurora, New York) and St. Mary's Seminary (Baltimore, Maryland). I am very appreciative of the enduring support, colleagueship, and encouragement I have received from the faculty and administration at St. Mary Seminary (Wycliffe, Ohio), with whom I am privileged to serve once again. From my co-workers in seminary ministry I have gained great insight into the interplay between spiritual and human formation.

The seminarians as well have also inspired me because they are often so genuinely eager to grow in spiritual maturity and to become truly holy men. Many of the men in priestly formation with whom I have worked have radiated a deep spiritual hunger and a pastoral zeal. To accompany them in their priestly formation has been one of the greatest privileges in my years as a priest. I am very grateful to God for what these men are now doing and will continue to do for the church.

My own service as the pastor at Holy Cross Church in Fairview, Pennsylvania, was a time of great learning for me that brought together in a more cohesive manner the human, intellectual, pastoral, and spiritual formation that had been continuing in my priesthood for many years. That learning and integration of all the aspects of priestly life and ministry now continues for me with the wonderful parish of St. John the Evangelist in Girard, Pennsylvania. The people of these two parishes comprise dynamic communities of faith, worship, and service. They demonstrate a spirited commitment to each other and a deep desire to grow in holiness and in the understanding of our Catholic tradition. Therefore, they have called forth in me the need to constantly develop an increasingly integrated life as a priest, one that meets their own human, intellectual, pastoral, and spiritual needs as the People of God. From them I have come to recognize that priesthood has to be lived in an authentically integrated way, and I began to think about writing on the topic.

In order to write this book, I lived for two summers at Mount Saviour Monastery in Pine City, New York. I could not have asked for a better environment in which to pray, reflect, and then consider the growth and struggles in the spiritual life. Prior John Thompson and the Benedictine monks at Mount Saviour were hospitable in every sense that their Father Benedict intended. I am deeply grateful for their prayerful support and encouragement.

I also need to thank the people at Liturgical Press. They made the whole process of my proposal becoming a manuscript becoming a published text quite manageable. They provided a tremendous amount of helpful assistance with the organization and clarity of what I was trying to convey.

In addition, I want to acknowledge my bishop, Most Rev. Lawrence Persico. From the moment I told him that my proposal for a book on priestly spirituality had been accepted for publication, he expressed tremendous delight and encouragement. For his support throughout the writing process I am deeply grateful.

Finally, I want to thank my brother, Fr. John Detisch, who has always provided me a home in Erie when I have been serving outside of the diocese in seminary work. He has continually made sure that I had a comfortable place to relax, read, write, and celebrate the Eucharist with a parish community.

Introduction

Once while Jesus was standing beside the lake of Gennesaret, and the crowd was pressing in on him to hear the word of God, he saw two boats there at the shore of the lake; the fishermen had gone out of them and were washing their nets. He got into one of the boats, the one belonging to Simon, and asked him to put out a little way from the shore. Then he sat down and taught the crowds from the boat. When he had finished speaking, he said to Simon, "Put out into the deep water and let down your nets for a catch." Simon answered, "Master, we have worked all night long but have caught nothing. Yet if you say so, I will let down the nets." When they had done this, they caught so many fish that their nets were beginning to break. So they signaled their partners in the other boat to come and help them. And they came and filled both boats, so that they began to sink.
—Luke 5:1-7

Finding the Deeper Stream

When I was a young boy my family vacationed regularly in Cook Forest State Park in Western Pennsylvania. We would take up residence in a cabin and spend several days exploring the beauty and intrigue of nature. My three brothers and I would exude all the youthful confidence (even arrogance) of mighty pioneers setting out to explore, discover, and then master the forces of the mostly untainted natural world. We took literally the words of the Creator to the first human beings: "[F]ill the earth and subdue it; and have dominion over the fish of the sea and over the birds of the air and over every living thing that moves upon the earth" (Gen 1:28).

1

On our very first excursion into the state park, on our very first day of setting out to "subdue" the natural world and master it, we all decided with great bravado to canoe down the Clarion River that runs through the center of the state park. Not only had none of us ever canoed before, but we were also completely unprepared for how shallow the river could get in the summer. Repeatedly one of our canoes would get stuck on a rock or mired in the mud of the riverbed. A few times we even had to get out of our canoes into the dirty, muddy water and make right our canoes that had gone terribly wrong. Angry words, harsh accusations, and lots of sibling name-calling transpired. By the time we reached the docks of the canoe rental place down the river, we had all had enough. In the end, the river subdued *us*. Needless to say, our enthusiastic but not well-informed adventure became a frustrating, unnerving, and calamitous experience. In subsequent trips to Cook Forest, we avoided canoeing at all costs, blaming the river for being too shallow but not wanting to admit our own incompetence.

Some years later, however, when I vacationed in the same state park with some friends, I met a regular park visitor who shared similar frustrations about canoeing. This all changed for him when he discovered the secret to the river. He told us to look for the darker colored stream in the midst of the river. That was where the water was deeper and more easily navigable. Plus, he told us to rent kayaks rather than canoes since they had flatter bottoms and less chance of getting caught on rocks or stuck in the mud. We took the man's advice and soon discovered that the way to enjoy paddling down the Clarion River was to find the deeper stream in its midst and make use of the right vessel. There were still a few frustrating shallow spots and annoying rock beds, but we were much more able to right our boats quickly and continue on an enjoyable adventure.

Because of this experience, "finding the deeper stream" has become for me an apt metaphor for my own spiritual biography as a priest—a narrative often mired in frustrations and failed endeavors in ministry; a story that often got stalled by the loss of motivation and inspiration in the midst of rocky situations; an account of priesthood that even devolved at times into anger and blaming of God, the church, and others for what had gone wrong. But once I was helped to begin to navigate the deeper streams of God's loving presence in my life and within myself, I traveled more easily through the adventures of priestly life and ministry and have been able to right what has gone wrong more quickly.

This image from my childhood has opened up for me some of the layers within the narrative of the call of the first disciples, often cited in both initial and ongoing priestly formation. The passage from Luke quoted above has much to say about the path of progress within the spiritual biography of seminarians and priests. When responding to the call of Jesus Christ eventually each person needs to hear the challenge to put out into deeper waters and discover how that deeper place is teeming with life. The response to this call needs to occur, however, from some place of familiarity in a person's life, as it did with these first disciples in their normal routine of fishing. Thus, the plunge into deeper waters exhibits both continuity and discontinuity within the spiritual life. In other words, from a place of comfortable regularity from which one has been fishing for a while, Christ will ask each disciple to go someplace unfamiliar, someplace further into the spiritual life—in short, someplace deeper. Furthermore, as with Simon and the others on the lake, to reap the benefits of putting "out into the deep water" one will most likely need the help of other companions who are also striving to do the same. Rarely are the disciples of Christ meant to navigate deeper waters on their own. But first, in their desire to follow Christ, disciples must recognize that the deeper waters even exist.

The process of "finding the deeper stream," as this book will trace, does not happen easily for the male ego that instinctively seeks success and the achievement of measurable results. Nor does the discovery happen merely through competent and capable functioning as a priest. An adage that I have come to use often with seminarians and priests in spiritual direction is this: *God will use all your gifts and abilities in ministry, but God will draw you closer to himself and deeper into yourself through your weaknesses and inabilities.* It is only when we get stuck on the rocks or mired in the messiness of priestly life that we are forced to find the deeper waters of priestly spirituality. When these difficult moments happen, some priests find the right companions in their lives to help them discover the deeper stream and reap the benefits of the life teeming within it. Other priests get stuck for a long time, mired in the messiness of their lives without any insight that near those muddy waters is a current that can flow into a much more navigable path in the spiritual life. They stay wedged in one place. And unfortunately there are other priests who, when their familiar path in the spiritual life does not work anymore, retreat into isolated frustration and often leave the stream altogether in anger and blame of others, never to return to the flowing waters of priestly spirituality.

From my own ministry with seminarians and priests over the years and from my own spiritual narrative, a pattern of gnawing questions and emotional conflicts can be identified. They can be expressed in the following ways:

- Even when we have the noblest motives, why does disappointment often become our undoing?

- Even when we have made tremendous personal sacrifices to say yes to God, why can it feel that God does not seem to notice?

- Even when our days are so full of doing good work, why can our nights often become so empty, lonely, or dreadful?

Perhaps the reader has wondered these same questions or others like them. As priests, we begin a vocational journey often striving to live what we see as an honorable calling and a fulfilling life; indeed, priesthood can be all this and more. But we have all seen so many enthusiastic good men leave priesthood so early. We have all known dedicated men find the daily life of ordained ministry too heavy a burden, as well as active, busy priests who seem to talk little of an inner life. Furthermore, we have all witnessed sincere servants of the Gospel develop dreadful habits of escapism and addictive gratification. Most likely, we have seen in ourselves one or more of these patterns. And yet in each of our dioceses and religious communities is a "cloud of witnesses" made up of priests who seem to have discovered a spiritual pathway that helps them navigate the rough waters. They have found the deeper stream. From my perspective, their testimony and biographies reveal three significant stages in developing the inner life of a priest that will be expounded upon in this text.

Introduction to the Three Stages of Archetypal Energy

The premise of this book is that the movement through these three stages happens through a graced shift in the archetypal energy—the undercurrent operating deep within the seminarian and priest—that is informing his sense of vocation, self-identity, and response to Christ's call. In their book, *King, Warrior, Magician, Lover: Rediscovering the Archetypes of the Mature Masculine*, Robert Moore and Douglas Gillette remind us of the Jungian concept of archetypes that are deeply at work within the unconscious and are manifested as "instinctual patterns and energy configurations . . . [that] provide the very foundations of our behaviors—our thinking, our feeling, and our characteristic human reactions."[1] Moore and Gillette echo the findings of many depth psychologists that "deep within every man are blueprints, what we call 'hard wiring,' for the calm and positive mature masculine."[2] Male archetypes abound and their influence on male spirituality is only beginning to be discovered and appreciated. What is very clear in depth psychology is that "different archetypes come on line at different developmental stages."[3] As human beings progress through life and mature, they do not lose their previously operative archetypes; instead they are assumed into a newer image-cluster that reshapes one's emotional, psychological, and spiritual patterns.

It is important to note that, from the viewpoint of Christian spirituality, archetypes are not mere psychological constructs, whether of the conscious or unconscious human mind. They also access the divine imprint placed within the core of each human being. Even the ancient spiritual guide Gregory of Nyssa recognized this. In his homily on the Beatitudes, Gregory reflects on the meaning of the beatitude "Blessed are the pure of heart." He recounts that "blessedness does not lie in knowing something about God, but rather in possessing God within oneself."[4] Gregory continues that, in the process of being purified, one "will regain likeness to his Archetype. . . . If he then looks into

1. Roger Moore and Douglas Gillette, *King, Warrior, Magician, Lover: Rediscovering the Archetypes of the Mature Masculine* (New York: Harper Collins, 1990), 9.
2. Ibid.
3. Ibid., 14.
4. Gregory of Nyssa, *Discourse Six on the Beatitudes* as quoted in "The Office of Readings" for Saturday, Week 12, in *The Liturgy of the Hours: The Roman Rite*, trans. International Committee on English in the Liturgy (New York: Catholic Book Publishing, 1975), 412–13. For the full text of the homily, see Anthony Meredith, *Gregory of Nyssa* (New York: Routledge, 1999), 91–99.

himself, he will see the vision he has longed for. This is the blessedness of the pure of heart: in seeing their own purity they see the divine Archetype mirrored in themselves."[5]

The process of being purified in the spiritual life and in priesthood not only brings a man closer to God but, in doing so, brings him closer to his True Self. This journey happens through a series of shifts from one form of archetypal energy within a priest to a newer one. These shifts are, however, normally occasioned by a conflict between a man's inner world and what he repeatedly encounters in the outer world, or at least how he interprets what he is experiencing in the outer world. In the flow of the spiritual life, this is when a seminarian or priest gets caught in the rocky current or gets stuck in waters that once flowed well but have now become too shallow to continue. These frustrating experiences can actually become key liminal moments in the spiritual biography of the seminarian and priest. Potentially, they can become the opportunities to heed the call of Christ to "put out into deep waters and lower your nets for a catch." When that call is heeded, then one brings his prayer and ministry, as well as his sense of self-identity and priestly vocation, into a deeper connection with Christ that will allow the man to cross the threshold into a stronger and richer spiritual life.

In my estimation, these liminal moments reveal how the many different archetypes operative in the male psyche coalesce into three main levels of energy when applied to the flow of priestly spirituality—three fathoms within "the deep," if you will. The first fathom is the strong current that draws the man into the water in the first place—to give his life for Christ in a way that will truly matter and genuinely make a difference. This is the Hero archetype, noted by many depth psychologists and anthropologists. The second fathom comes after repeated struggles in the strong current create a desire to find a more peaceful flow of life. This is when the priest learns to navigate the waters with Christ and no longer only for Christ or toward Christ. This stage brings together what I consider to be the dedicated Servant and Friend archetypes within a man. Finally, after further rough waters, the priest can sense that, even while striving to navigate life and ministry with Christ, the true generativity of his life will come from a place of communion—

5. Ibid., 413.

that place where he lives in Christ who lives in him. This is the third fathom; it arises out of the archetype of the Mystic, which others term the Sage or Spiritual Mentor archetype. These fathoms of archetypal energy within a man are three key stages in the spiritual development of priests, beginning when they are seminarians.

While the schema I will present traces a natural progression of archetypal energy from Hero to Servant to Mystic when a seminarian or priest enters more deeply into the spiritual life, the manner in which the grace of God operates is certainly not bound to my schema. While I am suggesting that the archetypal energies and the stages of development by which they manifest themselves are fairly typical in seminarians and priests, in no way can I make an absolute claim that they are normative. Not all seminarians and priests will identify with these archetypes as I characterize them or move through them exactly in the manner I am describing. Some may never advance to deeper levels of the spiritual life; some may begin at an already advanced stage. Nevertheless, because of the level of commonality that I have noticed in the progression of archetypal energy within seminarians and priests, I offer this explication of three stages within the spiritual life as fairly typical of most men in the years before and after ordination to the priesthood. At the very least, I hope the pattern of stages I put forth is helpful for seminarians, priests, formators, and spiritual directors to gain some insights into the connections between one's operative archetypal energies and how they become expressed in the spiritual and ministerial life of a priest or seminarian.

Stage 1 of this pattern can be called "A Noble Hero *for* Christ." I describe it as the coming to awareness, usually but not exclusively in young adulthood, that one wants to live his life for Christ. This is the flowing current—the more meaningful path—for a man whose religious consciousness has been awakened and who is captivated by the person of Jesus Christ and wants to do more than what other careers offer. At this stage, a sense of religious and priestly vocation awakens, leading a man to become a seminarian who is frequently filled with noble desire and enthusiastic zeal. This desire and enthusiasm often continue in the heady months and years after ordination. But when significant disappointment, frustration, loneliness, or even failure occurs, the man who is attentive to the interior life will recognize that a shift needs to occur inside of him. He has to "put out into the deep" and discover a way to live this noble life from a new place in the spiritual journey.

This is when stage 2 can set in, which I have titled "A Faithful Servant *with* Christ." The gallant desire to live the life of a priest becomes the more tempered recognition that one must do this not merely out of a motivation *for* Christ but from a desire to live *with* Christ, who is the priest's intimate and steadfast helper and guide. During this stage, the exercise of ministry arises out of the powerful awareness of the companionship of Christ, who is now given the chance to set the tone and the pathway for priestly life and ministry more vividly. Drawing from the steadfastness of the Hero archetype in the previous stage, the priest is able to navigate rough waters because he sees himself as one still committed to Christ but now as a Servant who is a friend and companion, as one by Christ's side, which is a shift in archetypal energy. After a while, however, even while ministering alongside Christ, gnawing pangs of continued loneliness and repeated ineffectiveness set in, and with them come feelings of regret or qualms about being unappreciated. All of these can make even the smallest space between a priest and his Divine Companion feel like a gaping chasm of disconnection and alienation. Something more, something deeper is needed. If a priest remains true to the spiritual life, especially in this rocky place where he can get mired in regret and become fixated on considerations of leaving the priesthood, an even deeper stream can be discovered, leading to the next stage.

In stage 3 the companionship of Christ is more fully revealed as the indwelling of Christ, who in turn calls the priest to dwell in him. In this stage the priest is invited to become "A Humble Mystic *in* Christ." At this point, a priest's noble desire to live *for* Christ and his faithful friendship *with* Christ becomes communion *in* Christ—the discovery of Christ's presence deep in one's core and the experience of one's apostolic ministry being lived out deep within the priestly heart of Christ. From this archetypal energy of Mystic the priest now experiences celibacy in a new way and sees it as truly generative "fatherhood." Furthermore, for the Mystic the ups and downs of ordained ministry are all experienced on some level as grace-filled; priesthood, in a freeing and wonderful way, is recognized not to be about the priest himself, who no longer needs it to be.

The narrative that follows will explore more fully each of these stages: *for* Christ, *with* Christ, and *in* Christ. While this book will focus on the spiritual path of priests, I certainly recognize that these stages may aptly apply in some way to many Christian men and women who have been devoted to the spiritual life and are engaged in apostolic ministry. I do not write this text in order to exclude or to diminish the depth of their inner lives. Because of my ministerial work in seminary formation, however, and my own inner work through my struggles and growth long after priestly ordination, I feel the particular need to help priests with their own ongoing formation and name for them what they might be experiencing in their spiritual narratives.

Purposes of This Book

With all this in mind, I offer this text for the following reasons. First of all, I am indebted to the priests who have inspired me and the spiritual guides whose insights have helped me to find the deeper stream and to keep putting out into that deep. Hopefully, the fruits of their labors will find expression in the pages that follow. Second, I want to assist seminarians and priests who have not yet found their true inner life, either still unsure about how to put out into the deeper water or thinking that what is deep within them is too difficult or cumbersome to navigate. Finding and exploring one's inner life as a priest happens in stages, since there are layers to one's depth. (This is true of everyone, of course, not just of priests.) It also does not happen automatically or without the assistance of spiritual guides who themselves have learned to navigate the deeper currents of ordained ministry. This biographical sketch of priestly life is meant to explore the significant stages in the discovery and development of a fuller inner life in those who respond to and then seek to live authentically the call of Christ to be a priest. It arises out of my own journey in the spiritual life as well as from the many grace-filled opportunities I have had to companion seminarians and priests in their spiritual development.

A third reason for writing this book is my hope that what I sketch as the contours of the spiritual biography of seminarians who become priests will assist those whose ministry either focuses on initial priestly formation programs in seminaries or overseeing programs of ongoing priestly formation in dioceses and religious communities. Neither arena is easy work, but both are always powerful and rewarding ministry. Much has been written to assist those in seminary formation work, but little has been offered regarding the ongoing formation of priests. It is my observation that many dioceses struggle with how best to implement an effective program of clergy continuing education and formation. Bishops, vicars for clergy, and priest personnel directors become quickly frustrated with the lack of cooperation, participation, and enthusiasm in their presbyterates for days of recollection. They are at a loss at times on how best to offer ongoing educational opportunities and how to attract priests to annual retreats that are comprised of more purposeful silence and reflection rather than mere enjoyable fellowship and recreation. Yet the ongoing intellectual, human, pastoral, and spiritual formation of priests must become and remain a priority in each diocese. It was St. John Paul II who made this clarion call in his pivotal apostolic exhortation *Pastores Dabo Vobis*, which addresses both initial priestly formation in seminaries and postordination priestly formation in dioceses and religious orders. The pope is very clear that the ongoing formation of priests is constitutive of the very nature of holy orders. In commenting on the reasons for ongoing priestly formation, St. John Paul states:

> We thus see that the proper foundation and original motivation for ongoing formation is contained in the dynamism of the sacrament of holy orders. Certainly there are also purely human reasons which call for the priest to engage in ongoing formation. This formation is demanded by his own continuing personal growth. Every life is a constant path toward maturity, a maturity which cannot be attained except by constant formation. It is also demanded by the priestly ministry seen in a general way and taken in common with other professions, that is, as a service directed to others. There is no profession, job or work which does not require constant updating if it is to remain current and effective. The need to "keep pace" with the path of history is another human reason justifying ongoing formation.[6]

It is, however, the pope's theological explanation for the need for ongoing formation of priests that reflects the deeper stream of spiritual growth and development within a priest. St. John Paul asserts:

> The sacrament of holy orders, by its nature (common to all the sacraments) as a "sign" may be considered, and truly is, a word of

6. Pope John Paul II, *Pastores Dabo Vobis*, Postsynodal Apostolic Exhortation, no. 70.

God. It is a word of God which calls and sends forth. It is the strongest expression of the priest's vocation and mission. By the sacrament of holy orders, God calls the candidate "to" the priesthood "coram ecclesia." The "come, follow me" of Jesus is proclaimed fully and definitively in the sacramental celebration of his Church. It is made manifest and communicated by the Church's voice, which is heard in the words of the bishop who prays and imposes his hands. The priest then gives his response, in faith, to Jesus' call. "I am coming, to follow you." From this moment there begins that response which, as a fundamental choice, must be expressed anew and reaffirmed through the years of his priesthood in countless other responses, all of them rooted in and enlivened by that "yes" of holy orders. In this sense one can speak of a vocation "within" the priesthood. The fact is that God continues to call and send forth, revealing his saving plan in the historical development of the priest's life and the life of the Church and of society. It is in this perspective that the meaning of ongoing formation emerges. Permanent formation is necessary in order to discern and follow this constant call or will of God.[7]

I would be very heartened to discover that the ensuing pages of text might help both seminaries and dioceses in their important and complementary tasks of initial and ongoing priestly formation. I hope that this text might help seminary formators and spiritual directors to name for seminarians the elements of priestly life in the years ahead and how to navigate the shifts that will happen inside of them down the road. Furthermore, perhaps this book can give some priests enduring very "dark nights" a ray of light and hope. Conceivably it can help those who have lost contact with their original motives for ordination to find even deeper and more enduring ones. And perhaps it can help those priests who feel the tug to work harder on their spiritual lives to recognize what concrete steps they might take toward attaining that goal.

A final reason for my writing this book needs some explanation; it is a desire for greater communion among priests. It has been no secret that many dioceses and religious communities are experiencing a generational divide that has not diminished in recent years, though the hope was that it would. What has been often described as the clash between "Vatican II priests" and "John Paul II" priests has become

7. Ibid.

even more exacerbated with what is now being called "the Francis effect" and what I have termed "the Benedict allegiance." This clash is most clearly evidenced in matters of liturgical style and preference, homiletic content and demeanor, as well as choices of clerical garb. In addition, priests and seminarians are caught between the maelstroms that have arisen as different ideologies compete for the definitive manner in which the Second Vatican Council should be interpreted. My hope is that by delving into the contours and texture of the nature in which priestly spirituality develops and grows all priests will see themselves and those with whom they disagree in the same boat. After all, every priest struggles at times and every priest begins the vocational journey with the same energy of noble enthusiasm and zeal. Likewise, every priest has been called to put out into the deep when gnawing questions or conflicted experiences arise.

Five Basic Principles

As the chapters in this book unfold, there are five basic principles that will be traced throughout. These form the framework of understanding the shifts that occur as a priest navigates the currents of the spiritual life from one archetype to the next.

First of all, the unavoidable experiences of disappointment, pain, brokenness, and emptiness ought to be regarded as grace-filled invitations to go deeper into the spiritual life of priesthood. While they may not feel like graced experiences, and they are not to be seen as caused by God, they need to be recognized as moments in which God has entered intimately in order to help each person "put out into the deep."

Second, in each stage it becomes clear that where a priest primarily locates the brokenness in life to which he is called to reach out ministerially—that is where the priest will most fully direct his spiritual energy and find his connection to Christ. For instance, we will see how the Hero, while recognizing he is a sinful human being himself, will primarily see sinfulness and brokenness "out there" to be remedied for Christ. He will see all the things wrong in the world and in people's lives from which he wants to help rescue them on behalf of Christ the Savior. In the next stage, the Servant primarily sees brokenness all around him and as a part of himself that is to be met and addressed with Christ's help. He knows that he is not going to end this brokenness but that he has a role in drawing all of it into a redemptive encounter with Christ. Furthermore, at this point the priest sees that the sinful and shattered nature of human life comes in very personal forms, in the lives of people he meets every day and in his own life as well. It is only as a man yoked to Christ that he could meet this brokenness and bring to others what Christ desires to bring to them. Finally, a priest's move into archetypal energy of the Mystic happens when he comes to the very humbling insight that brokenness is at his deepest core, never to be escaped; it is the place of deepest communion with Christ and the place from which he is to meet and minister to all other brokenness in others.

Third, in each stage the content and style of a priest's prayer will shift as he moves from one archetype to the next. While he may continue spiritual practices from the past, and is to remain true to his promises to pray the Liturgy of the Hours and celebrate the sacred mysteries, he may also discover that the manner in which he engages these practices has a different tone and quality to them. Furthermore, he may discontinue some forms of personal or devotional prayer and adopt different ones that prove to be more fruitful.

Fourth, while the priest is to keep the Eucharist at the center of his spiritual life, he will recognize that it beckons him onward in different ways in each stage of the journey. For instance, for the priest as Hero *for* Christ, the Eucharist finds its importance as the redemptive sacrifice of Christ offered on behalf of others (living and deceased); it is what the broken, sinful world needs from Christ. When he enters the stage of the Servant *with* Christ, the priest discovers that the Eucharist is the profound place of meeting Christ's real presence and companionship in the concreteness of human life. As this place of encounter, the Eucharist can transform lives, not only the priest's, but also the people whom he serves. Finally, when the priest recognizes his call to be a Mystic *in* Christ, the Eucharist reveals its significance as the broken Body of Christ and the poured out Blood of Christ in which all human brokenness finds redemptive communion. In the Eucharist, the priest's own broken self is intimately joined to Christ's self-gift and self-emptying, which in turn bolsters the priest's ability to guide his people toward eucharistic communion with Christ in their own brokenness.

Fifth, it is important to note that no matter where a seminarian or priest is within the stages of his own spiritual biography all the stages are within him to some degree. If he is truly open to the workings of God's grace and truly responding to the Christ's call to "put out into deep water," then even though he is operating out of one specific archetypal energy at the moment, the other energies are within him as well, summoning him to go deeper and enabling him to continue in the spiritual journey and in priestly ministry. Thus, each archetype is present from the beginning in different proportions of influence. Furthermore, as the priest moves from one stage to the next in the spiritual life, the previous archetypal energy is drawn into the deeper water and becomes operative in a different way within the new archetype. In other words, the aspects of each priestly archetype that are laden with grace will never be lost along the spiritual path.

As this text traces the stages of the spiritual path of priests, it will become evident how priestly spirituality engages the realities of the priest's humanity. The archetypal influences at the core of a priest's humanness are an important dimension of how God's grace often initially draws a man toward priesthood and then continually draws the priest deeper and deeper into the spiritual life, transforming his humanity along the way so that it becomes a clearer icon of the priesthood of Jesus Christ. In the "Catalog of Virtue" that Pope Francis offered as a Christmas address to the Curia in December 2015, he stated:

> Spirituality is the backbone of all service in the Church and in the Christian life. It is what nourishes all of our activity, sustaining and protecting it from human frailty and daily temptation. Humanity is what embodies the truthfulness of our faith: those who renounce their humanity renounce everything. . . . Spirituality and humanity, while innate qualities, are a potential needing to be activated fully, attained completely, and demonstrated daily.[8]

To that activation, attainment, and daily living out of the interplay between spirituality and humanity within the lives of seminarians and priests we now turn.

---

8. Pope Francis, "A Catalog of Virtue," in *With the Smell of the Sheep: The Pope Speaks to Priests, Bishops, and Other Shepherds*, ed. Giuseppe Merola (Maryknoll, NY: Orbis Books, 2017), 276.

CHAPTER ONE

A Noble Hero *for* Christ

I have called you by name, you are mine.
When you pass through the waters, I will be with you;
and through the rivers, they shall not overwhelm you.
—Isaiah 43:1b-3a

Awakening a Sense of Vocation

Vocation recruitment has become a high priority for every diocese. Many of the websites for vocation offices around the country have links to recruitment videos produced by different dioceses, religious organizations, and Catholic publishers. While each of these videos differs in content, they all have several common features: they evidence a professional quality of production, replete with stirring music and captivating images of healthy young men engaged in ministry; they feature seminarians and priests who appear to be excited and passionate about their vocation journey and their religious commitment; and they recount story lines of men who have felt "called by name" and now desire to give their lives to what they have discerned as the highest noble cause. The content of these videos captures well the nature of the initial stage of the spiritual life of a priest as seen in the lives of recently ordained men and young men in seminary formation exhibiting the energy of the first fervor of their commitment.

Bishop Robert Barron's *Word on Fire Catholic Ministries* has produced a video called "Heroic Priesthood." It focuses on what life is like in the seminary for men who are discerning priesthood, and it does this through the lens of several guys who enjoy playing basketball, which is used as a metaphor for the common pursuit of priesthood that binds these men together. In the video one seminarian describes how playing this sport allows him to stay physically fit and energetic so that he can take care of the gift God has given him—the call to priesthood. The seminarian remarks: "Now basketball is in service to the greatest good, is in service to God." His experience of the dedication and commitment needed for playing basketball allows this man to assert with great conviction about pursuing priesthood, "This guy Jesus, if you can muster the trust to follow him into the breach . . . you go there with him; there's glory on the other side. I believe that ordination and the years to follow will be filled with that glory."[1]

Another vocation recruitment video, titled "I Will Follow," features the powerful conversion stories of two men who are now priests. One of these priests, Mike, recounts his tremendous anger at the church when he was a young man, though he stayed connected to the church. Mike even became a lay missionary in Central America after college. While there, he remained angry and even openly mocked the local priest who served the mission. When Mike became deathly ill, though, this local priest immediately came to anoint him and comfort him. This experience set in motion a dramatic change of heart within the man, who eventually heard God's call to priesthood and responded with a definitive, "I will be your priest." As the video progresses, the now-ordained Fr. Mike is pictured in his ministry surrounded by young people eagerly attentive to what he is offering them. When the video returns to its interview of this priest, more of his thoughts about his vocation are shared. Fr. Mike states: "It is the most important thing I could do with my life. . . . As a father, as a priest, I get to heal God's children. As a father, as a priest, I get to feed God's children."[2]

Finally, perhaps the most emblematic video that portrays the call to priesthood as the noblest pursuit is one titled "Why Not Priest?" Featuring young men speaking several different languages, the video offers quick responses by these seminarians as to why they are pursuing priesthood. The following are some of the reasons they offer:

"Because when I die only what I've done for God counts."

"Because to follow Christ is the best adventure ever."

1. "Heroic Priesthood," *Word on Fire Ministries*, https://www.wordonfire.org/resources/video/heroic-priesthood/4432/.

2. "Will You Follow?," *Ascension Press*, http://willyoufollow.com/.

"Because God wants me to."

"Because one day I asked him what he wanted me to do."

"Because a lot of people don't know Christ as I do."

And most telling of all, "Because we need heroes."[3]

The videos described above, and others like them, are anything but subtle. They are direct, dramatic, and filled with stirring images, music, and narrative. Since these videos are geared toward the man who might be considering a call to priesthood, they appeal to that part of the man's consciousness that effectively engages his desire to do something magnanimous with his life. The producers of these videos are making a psychological "pitch" aimed at the element within a man's psyche—a man's ego energy—that stirs with a desire to live something very honorable, perhaps even something quite different from what he has been or is now currently living. They appeal to the Hero archetype.

Recalling that an archetype contains an amalgam of deep energies within a person, the priest as Hero also holds within it the desire within many seminarians and priests to be the upstanding father figure who magnanimously provides for the needs of his faith community (his priestly family) and confidently leads them to noble ends. The Hero also contains the desire to be the mighty prophetic teacher who will forthrightly challenge all that is wrong in the world and in society (which are often characterized as being overly secularized or even "godless") and teach the truths that will correct all the mistaken or misguided doctrinal and moral notions that people have.

While the ego energy exhibited at this Hero stage can be very evident and engaging in some men, it can be forceful, perhaps even brusque, in others. And in still other personalities it can be subtle and restrained. Regardless of the manner of expression, this ego energy is the necessary force that operates within the process of identity development in which individuals seek to discover their rightful place in the world. The "ego self," as many developmental psychologists and spiritual writers call it, is the product of each person's response to the most influential forces in the world around him or her by which a person comes to an individuated sense of self. It is at this point that a person decides, "This is who I want to be; this is what my life is to be about."

3. "Why Not Priest?," *Legionnaires of Christ*, https://www.whynotpriest.org/resources-1.

When seen within this context, the initial stage of priestly vocation often awakens amid a quest to discover the life a man now recognizes he is destined to live or, more accurately, is called to live. As with any noble quest, it is fueled by a desire to achieve an honorable goal, to accomplish a meaningful mission, and to become someone who can make a true difference in the lives of others. It is quite normal for a man emerging into adulthood to want his life to matter or for a man well into adulthood to discover at some point that his life could offer the world so much more. When a religious experience undergirds these moments of vocational awakening, a Christian man often concludes, "I want to live my life for Christ." Subsequently, some of these men further discern, "I want to become a priest for Christ, to do great things for the church and in the world on behalf of Christ." This is when a man is swept into the initial current of priestly spirituality, and it is a wonderful, exciting, but also daunting venture into the interior life and response to the call of Christ.

Recognizing a Mixture of Motives

At the beginning of the scriptural account of Simon Peter's commitment to Christ, he is a man of intensity, often getting it wrong more than he gets it right. Though he will be declared the rock of the church, at first Peter struggles with rather rocky and sometimes impetuous claims that he wants to follow a heroic notion of the Savior, presumably wanting to be that Savior's heroic disciple. For instance, Peter's notion of the messianic Savior does not allow him to accept that Christ should have to suffer (Mark 16:22), and he winces when his hero Jesus stoops down in the role of a household slave to wash his feet (John 13:8). When Christ speaks of his own impending death as well as Peter's forthcoming denial, Peter adamantly claims that he is willing to go to prison and to die for Christ (Luke 22:33). Eventually, tradition tells us, Simon Peter does heroically die as a martyr for Christ after being imprisoned in Rome during the time of Nero's persecution of the Christian community in the 60s of the first century AD. Peter's fascination with a heroic Savior and his desire to follow him valiantly might have begun with an ego energy that had not yet been fully transformed by the Spirit of Christ, but eventually this impetuous, strong-willed disciple, who sometimes got it wrong, in the end gets it very right.

As with the beginnings of Simon Peter's vocational story, in examining the first stage of a vocational journey, it is important for any seminarian or priest to probe as honestly as possible the mixture of motives that lies beneath the desire to live his life heroically for Christ. In our broken human condition, there are no such things as pure motives, only motives that need to be purified. All religious desire and longing is an amalgam of true selfless desire and lingering residue of self-interest or self-protection. This was true of Simon Peter; it is also true of all of us. As human beings, we simply cannot avoid this. Therefore, it is vital that a seminarian and later priest, along with his spiritual director, come to an accurate, honest, and forthright appraisal of the mixture of motives that lies within him. It is important for each of us to recognize that there are healthy sides of our operative archetypal energy but also unhealthy or undeveloped dimensions as well. Roger Moore and Douglas Gillette point out: "Human development does not always proceed so neatly . . . ; there are mixtures of the archetypal influences all along the way."[4] Healthy archetypal energy often surfaces in the nobler motives within us; the unhealthy archetypal energy often lurks within the unstated and self-protective instincts that try to keep certain dimensions of a person's character or personality in the shadows.

The more noble motives are often the stated ones. These are to be strengthened, honored, and celebrated (as well as featured in vocation promotional videos). The unstated motives, however, which are often less honorable and sometimes even unrecognized within a person's consciousness, must eventually come into the light so that they can be psychologically and spiritually integrated. If this is not done, these unstated but very operative motives will become the seeds of a priest's vocational undoing, whether in terms of wrongful behavior, an empty spiritual life, a pattern of self-absorbed habits, ineffective ministry, or a departure from priesthood.

Let us take a look at the most common operative motives that fuel a vocational desire to live one's life for Christ. They function on two levels: (1) the conscious, stated level and (2) the unstated level of motives a person may be conscious of or may not even recognize.

---

4. Roger Moore and Douglas Gillette, *King, Warrior, Magician, Lover: Rediscovering the Archetypes of the Mature Masculine* (New York: Harper Collins, 1990), 14.

Identifying the Stated, Conscious Level of Motives

In working with priests and seminarians in both the external forum of priestly formation and the internal forum of spiritual direction, the most commonly expressed motivations for entering the seminary and becoming a priest that I hear are different echoes of what were presented in the videos described earlier. Without the stirring music and vivid images of those videos, in undramatic but equally powerful conversations with seminarians and priests, I often hear them say things like:

- "I want to make a difference in people's lives."
- "I like helping people."
- "I want to give my life to God as completely as possible."
- "I enjoy going to Mass and helping in my parish so I see these interests as signs from God to be a priest."
- "I want more people to have Christ in their lives."
- "I want to do something that really matters."
- "I want others to get what I get out of practicing the Catholic faith."
- "I think it will be awesome to celebrate Mass and absolve people's sins in confession."
- "I want to give people the truth about Christ because so many people seem lost or without morals."
- "I think the church has the right answers to a lot of the deeper questions people are asking and I want to help share those answers by preaching the Word of God and teaching on behalf of the church."
- "I cannot ignore the tug I feel to become a priest and work for the church."

This list is not meant to be exhaustive but it captures the range of altruistic desires that express the religious, selfless, even at times zealous intentions often felt and stated in vocational discernment and decision making.

To encounter a seminarian or priest living out these motivations in a genuinely healthy and well-formed manner is a wonderful experience of grace. There is an energy exuded in the man's way of engaging in ministry that is as captivating as it is inspiring. This is a vocational lifestyle that truly portrays a "Noble Hero for Christ" because it can so often lead others to recognize the presence and action of Christ at work in their own lives through the ministry this man offers on behalf of the church.

Identifying the Unstated or Unconscious Level of Motives

When I have been privileged to work with a seminarian or priest in spiritual direction over a longer period of time, if he is someone willing to explore more fully the complexity of his inner life, another level of operative motives becomes clear. Some of these motives the man has been aware of and slowly brings to the light when an appropriate level of trust develops. Other unstated motives a man is not even aware of and does not recognize as operative within him for years, if ever. It usually takes a significant experience of heartache, disappointment, conflict, loneliness, or spiritual darkness to instigate a level of self-honesty and insight that makes these once unknown or unadmitted motives more clearly seen. The more "shame-based" a man is, however, and the more shameful he might feel about these other motives, the less likely he will be able to share them openly and honestly with another, including a spiritual director.

Even the most inspiring seminarian and captivating priest has within him deeper and sometimes darker motives that have developed over the years as the ego self's way of navigating the difficulties of life, dealing with any painful elements of one's childhood, or compensating for the missing elements in his perception of himself as a man in today's society. Unstated motives operate within every human being and most adults fail to integrate them in their self-awareness and in the way they invest themselves in the larger world. For seminarians and priests who live public exterior lives that are to be shaped by a well-grounded interior life, the failure to admit self-honestly and to examine directly these unstated motives can be disastrous. A forthright analysis of these unstated motives, however, often helps to lead a man to the next chapter of his spiritual biography (more on this in chapter 2).

What are some of the unstated or unrecognized motives for priesthood that a man may be aware of but often does not want to admit?

They are often discovered in a twofold manner. First of all, some seminarians and priests will eventually share their underlying operative motives with a formator or spiritual director when they have come to recognize these motives in themselves and have developed a level of trust that has made these men free enough to share what they have uncovered. Second, some underlying operative motives become apparent in formation or spiritual direction sessions as patterns that come to light through the self-reporting seminarians and priests offer, even if they have either not yet recognized these motives in themselves or not yet felt free enough to talk about them. These underlying motives often take the following shapes:

- "I am afraid of intimacy with another and so I don't have to worry about that with a celibate lifestyle."

- "I need to be important or gain recognition."

- "I have a compulsion to be right all the time and being a priest gives me that credibility and authority for people to accept what I am saying."

- "I come from a very unsettled experience of family life and so I have a strong need for 'belonging'; a priest always belongs to a community of people."

- "I could atone for my sinful past by becoming a priest."

- "I would please my religious parents/grandparents, who mean a lot to me, and make them very happy."

- "I do not want to disappoint those who keep telling me I should be a priest."

- "I am ashamed of my sexual energy/orientation, and celibacy would free me from the shame and struggle I am experiencing."

- "I have not done well in other careers/endeavors."

- "I think the struggles I have had in my life can help me to fix the problems in other people's lives."

- "I like the comfortable lifestyle I have seen some priests live."

None of these motives should be condemned in and of themselves by isolating them from the whole complex of drives within a man. Nor should any of them ever be dismissed. As mentioned already, they often arise out of the survival skills and defense mechanisms a man developed as he moved from childhood into adulthood bruised by the realities of his broken human condition but also shaped by a noble religious instinct within him that could not be ignored. Within the interplay between the stated and the unstated motives, the instinct arising from the mature Hero archetype often clashes with the needy Child archetype who instinctively seeks affirmation, security, protection, and attention.[5]

Fostering the Prayer Life of First Fervor

Underneath all the operative motives mentioned above is a religious instinct that nudges a man toward a priestly vocation. It stems from the same instinct that awakens the desire to become a spiritual person. While it is true that no one's spiritual biography is dictated by some preconceived script, there are certain patterns of prayer that emerge in each chapter of priestly life and ministry, including the all-important foundational one. In this initial period, exterior enthusiasm, zeal, and dedication are the evidence of a seminarian's or priest's interior captivation with the heroic ministry, death, and resurrection of Christ. These virtues also give witness to an interior recognition that it is very worthwhile for a man to give his life to the mission of the church. The seminarian or priest has come to the conclusion, "This is where I belong; this is what I ought to be doing." This spirituality of Christ-centeredness and church-committedness places the man in a relationship of giving himself to what he has discerned as the ultimate "Other" worthy of his life's energy. This "Other" is both Christ and his church who stand before the man as the beckoning icon of what his life ought to be. On days of heightened spiritual awareness, the man awakens in the morning hoping to see in the mirror a worthy representative of Christ and an effective minister of the church. At night, he hopes to retire to bed with the sense of contentment over what he has accomplished that day. This is what comprises the first fervor of a faithful seminarian and priest.

Since the archetypal energy of this stage of spiritual development often seeks to accomplish something for Christ and for the church, this

---

5. See Moore and Gillette, *King, Warrior, Magician, Lover*, 13–33.

same energy is seen in the seminarian's or priest's approach to his prayer life. During first fervor, there is a pronounced dedication to "accomplishing" prayer in order to fulfill what is expected of him by Christ and the church. To this end, a seminarian or priest will routinely engage in different acts of prayer: reciting the rosary; reading and praying the Divine Office; doing spiritual reading, often focused on the heroic lives of saints; engaging in devotional practices, especially those that reconnect him with a prior religious experience that was pivotal in his own vocational awakening; doing *lectio divina*, often with the goal of gaining insight for preaching; and trying to succeed at developing a true holy hour spent meditating before the Blessed Sacrament, which is frequently regarded as the true achievement of spiritual success. In addition, after ordination, the priest will also see his role in the Eucharist as vital to his spiritual life. At this initial stage that role is often described as "offering the Sacrifice of the Mass" on behalf of the church for others or "drawing others into an awesome liturgy that transforms their faith"; again, the imagery of a heroic enterprise dominates his spiritual and theological interpretation of what the Eucharist is.

In addition, the Blessed Virgin Mary as a true hero of commitment to Christ often figures prominently at this time. She is regarded as a powerful source of inspiration for dedicating one's life completely to Christ and giving oneself to God in noble chastity. Pope Francis appeals to this devotion to Mary in priests when he calls them to the grace of "apostolic audacity." He states:

> We humbly and confidently ask Our Lady for this grace—she who has been called "the first evangelizer." . . . She is the first to experience interiorly the joy of setting out to evangelize and to participate in the unprecedented audacity of the Son and of contemplating and proclaiming how God "has shown strength with his arm; he has scattered the proud in the thoughts of their hearts. He has brought down the powerful from their thrones, and has lifted up the lowly; he has filled the hungry with good things, and sent the rich away empty." From this audacity of Mary we are invited to participate as priests of the holy Church."[6]

6. Pope Francis, "The Grace of Apostolic Audacity," in *I Ask You, Be Shepherds: Reflections on Pastoral Ministry*, trans. Michael O'Hearn (New York: Herder and Herder, 2015), 35.

The attraction to this apostolic audacity fuels the Hero archetype of seminarians and priests in first fervor. The spiritual practices adopted to achieve this audacity are chosen because they are more easily measured as successful than are other forms of prayer, and they provide a stronger sense of being anchored in the things of God. In striving to find that strong anchoring and to develop a genuine prayer life, a man can point to these practices and say to himself with affirming satisfaction things like: "I was able to get in all of my prayers today that I have promised to pray"; "The time I spent before the Blessed Sacrament is getting closer to a true holy hour"; "My experience of *lectio divina* brought me some good insights." In this all-important first chapter of the spiritual biography of a priest, what is measurable, attainable, and tangible is far more valuable than other spiritual practices that might develop later that would lead a person into the ineffable and mystical dimensions of the spiritual life.

A man's commitment to achieving a better spiritual life at this first stage helps to embed within his inner spirit the inviolable need for prayer and the importance of developing a deeper sense of communion with Christ. These graces will serve him well in the later chapters of his spiritual biography, especially when the affective experiences of affirmation in prayer and ministry become conflicted or begin to wane, signaling the beginning of the end of first fervor.

Concurrent with the spiritual practices mentioned above, the Noble Hero for Christ will often discover during his reflection time an intense scrutiny of his behavior and attitudes, often revealing his faults and failings. The seminarian or priest can become acutely aware of how, where and when he has fallen short of being a true icon of Christ or a completely noble servant of the church. If the man regularly celebrates the sacrament of reconciliation with an insightful confessor, he may begin to discover the grace of God's abiding love for him even when his behavior, habits, inclinations, or dispositions have not been noble or appropriate. He may eventually come to recognize God's love as the *starting point* of his repentance and confession, not its result. Likewise, he may begin to sense that he is called to experience the constancy of God's love and mercy, not only when he has done good or great things for Christ and for the church, but even when the seminarian or priest gets things very wrong. This deepening awareness will become the seeds for the new chapter in his spiritual biography, for it will carry the man from the prior stage of wanting to accomplish a heroic spiritual and ministerial life for Christ and for the church to the beginnings of the next stage in which he will have to find a way to stay committed to prayer and ordained ministry once he recognizes that he will never quite be the hero he was hoping to be.

Dealing with Disappointment and Facing One's Own Limitations

In my diocese we regularly celebrate the significant ordination anniversaries of priests during our annual presbyteral convocation. A few years after I was ordained, a priest representing that year's silver jubilarians preached at the Jubilarian Liturgy. He and his classmates were ordained at the beginning of the Second Vatican Council. In his homily, this jubilarian commented on the manner of seminary training he received in the preconciliar years and then quite accurately stated that he had "been ordained for a church that ceased to be." As I listened to his words, I began to recall the exciting vision of church that I experienced in my seminary years, which took place two decades after the council. By that time so much of the ecclesiology and theology of priesthood within the conciliar documents had found its way into seminary classrooms and formation programs. I recollected how a great deal of what I learned seemed filled with tremendous hope and wonderful possibilities for what the church could be and how a priest could minister within that church. My early years of priesthood, however, were marred by the harsh realization that the theological vision I had learned and had been formed in had not yet come to pass and did not seem likely to occur anytime soon. In contrast to the jubilarian's comments, I said to myself with more than a little sadness in my heart, "I've been trained for a church that has yet to be."

From our perch of idealistic certitude, my classmates and I looked at the pastors to whom we were assigned and noticed that they seemed excited about the vision of Vatican II but struggled with how best to go about doing it. Often they had to contend with forceful malcontents who were still angry about the changes in the church after Vatican II. For these malcontents "Vatican II" was a term used in derision. Their anger was something for which my classmates and I were quite unprepared. It was dispiriting for us. Furthermore, we were imbued with a confidence that Vatican II was truly inspired by the Holy Spirit and that same Spirit was calling us to live out priestly ministry from the conciliar tenets of collegiality, subsidiarity, empowerment of lay ministry, dynamic preaching, fostering liturgy and sacramental ritual that was engaging, and advocating for social justice. We could not understand how good Catholic parishioners could oppose these principles or have a disinterest about them. Nor could we fathom how competent priests could minister in a manner different from what we were taught as all-important principles. (How's that for ministerial hubris on our part?) In response to all of this, there were at times anger, resentment, complaining, and friction with pastors and other priests. In those early years of ordained ministry, some classmates became very bitter; others requested a transfer to a new assignment; a few left priesthood. Eventually those who stayed within active ministry had to realize that noble idealism and harsh reality will always inevitably confront each other no matter what the profession, the moment in history, or the place of assignment. The challenge was to develop a healthy balance that allowed the ideals that truly reflected the will of God to be expressed appropriately in the concrete realities of our priestly ministry. Trying to develop this balance was where the need to return to prayer over and over again came into play. Without that prayer, we noticed how our inner life and our outward enthusiasm for priesthood fell apart. Within our prayer an undefined experience of some deeper reality beckoning us from inside of us began to emerge. It would take some time before that inchoate experience developed into a new level of a personal relationship with Christ (described in the next chapter).

Every newly ordained priest (and not so newly ordained) will eventually come up against harsh disappointments about the concrete realities of priestly life and ministry vis-à-vis the ideals of priesthood he has carried inside of him up to and after ordination. Furthermore, he will have to face the painful recognition that he is not able to do well everything expected of him; perhaps some things he might not even enjoy doing at all. This is when first fervor ends and can either lead to a deeper current of spiritual growth and priestly life or get mired in disillusion, despair, perhaps even leading to departure from the priesthood.

Not even the disciples of Jesus were immune from this. They too had first fervor and then experienced a loss of that fervor after Jesus

sent them out on mission in pairs. Luke's gospel recounts how, when
the disciples got their first taste of doing ministry on Christ's behalf,
they experienced great joy and excitement over being able to expel
demons in his name (Luke 10:17). Matthew's gospel, however, also
adds to the portrait of the disciples' initial foray into ministry a moment in which they succumbed to confusion and bewilderment over
their inability to expel the demon in a young boy. For this, Jesus even
castigates them: "Then the disciples came to Jesus privately and said,
'Why could we not cast it out?' He said to them, 'Because of your little
faith'" (Matt 17:19-20). In a further mission of being sent by Jesus as
emissaries to Samaria to prepare the people for Jesus' arrival, the fervor
of some of these disciples turned to anger, as evidenced in James and
John, who were aptly named "sons of thunder." When the people re-
fused to receive Jesus, James and John ask for permission to call down
fire from heaven upon them. But their comment and indignation earn
a stern rebuke from Jesus (see Luke 9:54-55).

Every priest dealing with disappointment can easily become a "son
of thunder," angrily casting blame on the people and situations that
are not receiving well what he has been absolutely convinced he has
been sent by Christ to do. The important ideals of which the zealous
man is firmly convinced could include the theology he has been taught
and excited about, the sense of the church's mission that he sees as
indispensable at the moment, the rules and regulations of the church
that he has accepted and tried to adhere to wholeheartedly, the style
of liturgy that he enjoys the most, the devotional practices that have
come to mean a lot to him, the moral precepts and analysis of social
and political issues that he regards as the only true way to approach
things. A rigid stance in these aforementioned areas has all the ingredients for vocational collapse or ministerial malpractice. Any priest
with a good sense of insight will recognize that he cannot go on with
such thunderous and self-righteous indignation. Hopefully, he will
come to recognize that rigidity, vehemence, and self-righteous indignation are features of the unhealthy shadow side of the Hero archetype.
All archetypes have their healthy, positive side and their negative
shadow. When the shadow surfaces, the priest will need to acknowledge it and be aware of its effects in his temperament. He will then
need to take all this (including his anger, frustration, and disappointment) into his prayer so as not to abandon prayer, which often happens

at this juncture because the negative shadow will try to block out the light that comes from prayer and insight.

Equally dangerous to a priestly vocation is when a priest turns the shadow side of the Hero in on himself. He cannot let his anger, frustration, and disappointment distort his once-noble self-giving to Christ into toxic self-blaming that is far from the heart of Jesus. This is when a man will have to pray about his own shortcomings and limitations, learning to accept the realities of his true creatureliness as God does and let go of an idealized version of himself. The priest will need to seek communion with Christ in the midst of his failings and mistakes and not regard his personal limitations as limitations on Christ's desire to continue to use his life for the sake of the Gospel.

A final peril that each priest needs to avoid is the compensatory behavior that can often arise at the time when anger, frustration, and disappointment dominate a man's temperament. Working through the anguish of this stage is hard work. It requires a significant amount of "tunneling" into the interior life. For those priests unaccustomed to such depth and rigor with the interior work or for those men more predisposed to seeking out quick, easy fixes in their lives, what can emerge is a pattern of seeking hurried relief from their anguish by engaging in overeating, significant alcohol consumption, gambling, self-indulgent purchasing of personal items, online addictions, and even sexual encounters.

Navigating the Spiritual Needs of the Afflicted Hero

What is vital for a priest to realize as his first fervor begins to fade (or suddenly evaporates) is that he cannot reject all that has stirred within his religious life up to that point. Spiritual and psychological growth is an organic process that cannot and will not happen all at once. Prior stages must be regarded as grace-filled steps toward each subsequent stage; they ought not to be dismissed with scorn, shame, or derision. Nor can a priest condemn those who have different religious stirrings or are at earlier stages of religious growth. Hopefully, a priest at this point will be able to surrender to Christ in prayer all the ingredients within his interior mind, heart, and will that were captivated enough by Christ to emerge as the vocational desire to be a Noble Hero for Christ and his church. By surrendering all these interior elements in prayer, the priest can open himself up to discover what Christ's Spirit now seeks to do in his interior life, especially with the "absolute" principles, the firmly maintained priorities, the long-held dreams and desires, the personality traits and disposition that have made this man the priest he now is. By entering deeper into a mode of prayer that listens to the stirrings of Holy Spirit inside of him and by engaging in spiritual direction that seeks to discover the wisdom of the Holy Spirit in a mentor or spiritual director, the priest can come to admit and hand over to the Lord whatever inside of him now needs to be reexamined, reappraised, and reconstituted on a different level of heroic commitment to Jesus Christ. The spiritual needs of the priest at this stage are to lead him to the resources that can, in the words of St. Paul to Timothy, "rekindle the gift of God that is within" (2 Tim 1:6).

For God's gift of a priestly vocation to be enkindled, it is crucial that the man engage in three key spiritual practices: (1) seeking out spiritual direction; (2) making a yearly silent, directed retreat; and (3) joining a priest support group, but one in which the men are willing to talk about the interior life and not just conduct a communal gripe session about the difficulties of priestly life or their current assignments. These practices have been pivotal in my own spiritual growth and the necessary rekindling of my sense of vocation. Without all three of these commitments in place, I know I would never have been able to endure or negotiate the vicissitudes of priestly life, especially the difficult and painful periods. When a seminarian or priest seeks me out for spiritual direction, I tell him very early on in the relationship that I want him eventually to include the other two elements of priestly spiritual nourishment as well, if they are not already in place. For me all three elements remain important because each one helps to clarify and deepen different aspects of priestly spirituality.

First of all, meeting with a spiritual director on a regular basis always forces a priest to a level of self-honesty about what is stirring inside of him, what lies beneath his behavior and decisions, and how he may or may not be hearing God in his prayer. By articulating to a trusted listener the content of one's inner life, that content can be revealed more clearly to the man himself, including the operative motives he may not yet have acknowledged or integrated and that may be undermining his true self-giving in priesthood. In spiritual direction, the patterns and pitfalls, the graces and grievances of one's inner life become more acutely recognized and known. In addition, the reflective listening and the sage advice of a good spiritual director can offer two key components for spiritual growth: affirmation of the ways a man· is in sync with God, and challenge about what he might be distorting or ignoring in his assessment of what is going on inside of him and in his priestly life and ministry.

For any priest dealing with disillusionment, the importance of spiritual direction cannot be understated. I would go so far as to conclude that such a priest without a spiritual director risks the danger of experiencing vocational collapse and engaging in grave ministerial malpractice. In spiritual direction a priest can find a new clarity of motivations. Perhaps the heretofore unacknowledged and unexamined operative motives can be recognized by a priest as he trusts and listens to the objective perspective a spiritual director can bring. That objectivity can help a priest identify which motives might need to be more honored, which ones ought to be discarded, and which ones could perhaps be reshaped so as to be more fitting with the real features of priestly life. Furthermore, the priest's self-reporting to his spiritual director about the content of his prayer can lead to a more accurate attentiveness to what God's voice is speaking and how God might be seeking to claim more fully some of the operative motives and transform other ones. The amalgam of motives that stirred as a desire to be a Hero for Christ within a man moving toward ordination might now need to be reconstituted by Christ as a different kind of motivating energy inside of him.

A second imperative for priests dealing with the frustrations and disappointments of priesthood is to make a yearly silent, directed retreat. It was my spiritual director in seminary who encouraged me to make such a retreat because it would help me to delve deeper into my interior life with Christ much more than a group retreat would. Only the paired graces of protracted silence and a capable director can assist in this inner journey most effectively. My experiences of Ignatian-style retreats over the years have revealed this to me. In such a retreat, engaging in the Ignatian method of imaginative prayer with a Scripture passage often allows the pray-er to hear and see Christ drawing him toward deeper communion with Christ in ways that even regular prayer throughout the year has not always allowed. The fruits of silent, directed retreats can allow a priest to embrace the reality of his life and his personhood with greater freedom from regret, resentment, or the desire to have had a different life. This in turn allows the retreatant to discover how to give his life away in a way that is more truly expressive of his real self—the self that God has always known and loved and not the self that he thought he had to become in order to warrant God's love. Those of you who are familiar with the Spiritual Exercises of St. Ignatius of Loyola will recognize this grace as the fruit of the First Week of the Exercises, in which the retreatant is called to ponder his or her creatureliness as total gift of love from the Creator. Furthermore, it is from the fundamental acceptance of the Creator's love that the retreatant can then more fully acknowledge his or her sinfulness, brokenness, and utter need of God's mercy. This is the all-important sacred gift that keeps the disillusioned Hero from sinking into despair.

Additional retreat graces from God that one can experience on silent, directed retreats can include the ability to recognize and confront some of one's inner demons, the capacity to receive God's love more fully, the clarity to see which specific dimensions of one's current ministry are in sync with God and which are not, the discernment of new types of ministry to which one might be called, and the reaffirmation of Christ's desire that a man be a priest for God and for God's People. Only in silence can the intimate voice of Christ be heard inside of us, revealing the love of the Father and the desire of the Father for our lives. Only in silence can the authentic stirrings of the Holy Spirit be recognized and distinguished from other desires that may not really be of God. Likewise, only with a capable director can we gain true insight about what the voice is saying and where the stirrings are leading so that we are not misled by the hurting or disappointed ego energy inside and do not unintentionally move away from what the Father asks of us and needs from us. In commenting on the need for ongoing spiritual formation of priests after ordination, St. John Paul II writes in *Pastores Dabo Vobis* about a priest's prayer life:

> The priest's prayer life in particular needs to be continually "re-formed." Experience teaches that in prayer one cannot live off past gains. Every day we need not only to renew our external fidelity to times of prayer, especially those devoted to the celebration of the Liturgy of the Hours and those left to personal choice and not reinforced by fixed times of liturgical service, but also to

strive constantly for the experience of a genuine personal encounter with Jesus, a trusting dialogue with the Father and a deep experience of the Spirit.[7]

The trinitarian encounter in prayer that St. John Paul describes is perhaps the greatest benefit of a yearly silent, directed retreat. The vividness of prayer experiences on such retreats contains graces for a priest's prayer life throughout the year, especially as he strives to hold on to his noble assent to the call of Christ while enduring the difficulties and disappointments that priestly life can have at times. This kind of prayer gently moves the priest out of the prior ego energy in which the operative questions were: "What do you ask of my life, Lord?" and "How is my life to continue to be given for you?" Now the priest, in the cauldron of anguish and doubt, can begin to discover in his prayer experiences a different question: "Lord, how are you and I to be priests together?" The yearly encounters with deep silence fuel the kind of prayer that can enter this cauldron and not be undone by it.

The third imperative in the ongoing spiritual formation of priests is becoming a member of a priestly support group that is willing to engage in true faith sharing, honest self-reporting about one's life and ministry, and silent prayer in communion with each other, perhaps before the Blessed Sacrament. My own experience with Jesus Caritas groups has been a vital source of encouragement and insight regarding priestly life and ministry. Furthermore, my Jesus Caritas experiences have assured me over and over again that the difficulties and struggles I sometimes face are not unique to me. We priests are struggling and dealing with difficulties *together*, and that has made all the difference to me. I cannot describe adequately enough what it feels like every time I have prayed with my brother priests Charles de Foucauld's heroic words of surrender:

> Father, I abandon myself into your hands;
> do with me what you will.
> Whatever you may do, I thank you:
> I am ready for all, I accept all.

7. Pope John Paul II, *Pastores Dabo Vobis*, Postsynodal Apostolic Exhortation, no. 72.

Let only your will be done in me,
and in all your creatures—
I wish no more than this, O Lord.

Into your hands I commend my soul:
I offer it to you with all the love of my heart,
for I love you, Lord, and so need to give myself,
to surrender myself into your hands without reserve,
and with boundless confidence,
for you are my Father.[8]

The key to the successful support group for priests is that each member makes it a top priority and that each member understands the true nature of the gathering—to share faith, hope, and wisdom as priests whose lives are centered in the person of Jesus Christ, the true High Priest. While there need to be wonderful opportunities for the building up of friendship and priestly fraternity within the sessions, the main focus must remain the faith sharing by the members of the group in trust and respect with each other about how and where each one has been feeling in sync with Christ in his priestly life and ministry and how and where each one has not. This allows mutual experiences of disillusionment and doubt to be brought into the light where they are revealed for what they are—invitations for the moments of feeling disconnected to become opportunities for deeper growth in one's relationship with the Lord. At the same time, the sharing in trust and respect about the realities of his priesthood also prevents each man's frustrations and doubts from becoming what they are not—signs that all along he should never have been ordained or that Christ has misled him. During the most difficult times in ministry, there is nothing more healing than the encouragement and support of other priests who, in revealing their own struggles, evidence their deeper fidelity to Christ and thereby summon forth that heroic fidelity from each other.

In a healthy and life-giving support group of priests, the Noble Hero is no longer portrayed as the highly enthusiastic man of intense conviction who feels utterly fulfilled in all that he is doing for Christ and

8. This prayer as well as information about Jesus Caritas communities can be found at http://www.jesuscaritas.info/.

for the church. Instead, the Noble Hero has been transformed by the clash between ideals and reality—by the loss of first fervor—into the steadily faithful Servant who continues to offer to the People of God what Christ asks of him. Within a support group of such faithful men, the Hero for Christ is no longer depicted as the handsome and athletic man who speaks with eloquence and certitude in promotional videos about his call from Christ but the scarred Servant whose sometimes unsteady voice speaks of the doubts he has had about his vocation and then, with an even more humbled voice, shares how Christ has reaffirmed his vocation in newer and deeper ways.

Finding the Hero's Deeper Stream in the Spiritual Life

The priest who remains faithful to prayer, engages regularly in spiritual direction, and seeks out the support of healthy, committed priests will be able to find the deeper stream in his spirit that will allow him to navigate more easily through the rough waters of disillusionment and despair. At the same time, the priest will need to be attentive to the ways that God is seeking to bring consolation into his life and to affirm his vocation. There will always be parishioners who appreciate what a priest has to offer and will let him know that. Just when a priest's despair makes him feel like he is only going through the motions of pastoral ministry, there will be a pastoral visit to the sickbed of someone who will grab the priest's hands and express with deep gratitude how much it meant that he came to visit. Just when the priest begins to hear his own preaching sound hollow and perfunctory, there will be a parishioner at the doorway on Sunday after liturgy saying, "Father, in your homily today you said exactly what I needed to hear." Just when a priest becomes enervated by a loss of enthusiasm and zeal, a parishioner will send a card thanking him for all that he does for the parish. These moments of "coincidental grace" can become a new awakening within the priest when it begins to dawn on him that his heroism stems not merely from what he externally does for Christ and for the church but from what Christ seems to be doing through him and for him, even—perhaps especially—when the priest does not feel very heroic. That insight is the key to discovering the deeper stream.

In his book *Falling Upward: A Spirituality of the Two Halves of Life*, Richard Rohr describes the stages that the hero or heroine must pass through in order to become the truly generative person he or she is meant to be. One of those necessary stages, Rohr remarks, is when the hero or heroine experiences overwhelming difficulty in his or her mission. Rohr states: "He or she 'falls through' what is merely *his or her life situation* to discover his or her *Real Life*, which is always a much deeper river, hidden beneath the appearances. Most people confuse their life situation with their actual life, which is an underlying flow beneath the everyday events."[9] For a priest, this "much deeper river" creates a shift from finding satisfaction in the external successes of ministry to finding consolation in the internal companionship of Christ.

In addition, once the priest enters the "underlying flow" he cannot really ignore its movement when he prays or ponders. It will seek to draw all the operative motives above it down into its current so that what emerges within a man's heart, mind, and spirit is a desire to be a priest that integrates more fully all that his genuine creatureliness is about—his abilities and his limitations, his noble and his not-so-noble desires, the self-giving and the self-protective drives of his psyche's archetypes, the celebrated and the concealed intentions that are in his inner life. Furthermore, this discovery of the deeper stream will eventually demand different forms of personal prayer because this integration of his total self is not a self-accomplished feat of attaining measurable results. Prayer will now be done less *for* Christ and more so *with* Christ, who constantly seeks to draw each person more fully into the Father's embrace and to reveal how the Father sees each of us and what the Father asks of us. Thus, a priest's prayer life at this time will eventually need to shift away from only the recitation and accomplishment of prayer to include more efforts at listening and cooperating.

Moreover, the priest will discover through this deeper stream that the angst, disillusionment, and discontentment he has been experiencing have meaning and value. They all comprise an experience of sharing in a "paschal death" with Christ. Shakespeare's Julius Caesar claims that "a coward dies a thousand times before his death, but the valiant taste of death just once."[10] From the perspective of the paschal mystery, the opposite is actually true, which means that the heroic priest dies

9. Richard Rohr, *Falling Upward: A Spirituality for the Two Halves of Life* (San Francisco: Jossey-Bass, 2011), 19.
10. *Julius Caesar*, act 1, scene 2, line 32.

many deaths. Ronald Rolheiser describes well the necessity and the experience of paschal deaths for each person drawn into the underlying flow of the spiritual life. In his wonderful and well-received treatise on the fundamentals of Christian spirituality, *The Holy Longing*, Rolheiser traces the elements of the "paschal cycle" that every genuine disciple of Christ will eventually need to recognize and embrace at important transformative moments in his or her life. This paschal cycle involves the Good Friday moment of a death of something inside of us or in our lives that has been very important. This in turn is followed by the resurrection of something new but not yet fully experienced. The experience of the new cannot happen until we pass through a true period of mourning of what has been lost. This is the "forty days after Easter" period. When we can finally let go of what we have lost by letting it bless us (the Ascension moment), then soon the spirit of the new reality will rush into our interiority and enable us to live it out with great joy (the Pentecost moment).[11]

There are many kinds of "paschal deaths" that will occur in each person's life. Among them Rolheiser lists the following: the death of our youth; the death of our wholeness (accepting that we are broken, limited persons); the death of our dreams (mourning our incompleteness); the death of our honeymoons (our romantic or zealous levels of commitment); the death of idealized notions of our families and our personal histories; the death of certain ideas of God, church, etc.[12] What allows those deaths to become "paschal" and, therefore, redemptive and meaningful is a genuine search for their connection to Christ's own paschal mystery. The deeper stream will always include the paschal mystery of Christ. By entering this stream the once-enthusiastic-but-untested priest will come to recognize that his idealized image of the priest-Hero-for-Christ now has to die so that he can receive from Christ a "paschal resurrection" of a newer and deeper sense of how he can live his life nobly for Christ as a priest. The experience of this paschal death of the Hero involves true grief, for it comes from the painful experiences of disillusionment, anger, and despair already detailed in this chapter.

11. Ronald Rolheiser, *The Holy Longing: The Search for a Christian Spirituality* (New York: Doubleday, 1999), 147–48.
12. Ibid., 148–62.

It is crucial that the prayer life of the priest experiencing a paschal death allows the proper time for grieving and does not seek to gloss it over, circumvent it, or hasten its duration. Instead, hopefully, the priest will bring up what he is experiencing to a spiritual director, who can help the man to identify accurately what he is experiencing and then discover how to express the grief of his "death" in prayer. It is in moments like this that the priest needs to persist in his previous pattern of devotion to the prayer that is expected of him by the church, for healing and strength are found within those practices. In particular, he can experience how the words of the psalms and canticles, which are a part of the Divine Office, take on a certain resonance through what is being expressed. For instance, in the canticle of Hezekiah (Isa 38:10, 12-14) during Tuesday Morning Prayer, Week 2, the once afflicted king describes the despair he once endured:

> Once I said:
> "In the noontime of life I must depart!
> To the gates of the nether world I shall be consigned
> for the rest of my years . . . "
>
> My dwelling, like a shepherd's tent,
> is struck down and borne away from me;
> you have folded up my life, like a weaver
> who severs the last thread.
>
> Day and night you give me over to torment;
> I cry out until the dawn.
> Like a lion he breaks all my bones;
> Day and night you give me over to torment.[13]

In Psalm 77:1-10 (prayed during Wednesday Morning Prayer, Week 2), the psalmist captures well the process of anguish that one experiencing a paschal death needs to endure. It is a process that includes an aching nostalgia for what once was but no longer is. The psalmist's

---

13. Because of the frequency and familiarity with which a seminarian or priest prays with the current edition of the Psalms and Canticles in the Liturgy of the Hours, all of the texts from the Liturgy of the Hours in this book are taken from the International Commission on English in the Liturgy translation of *The Liturgy of the Hours* (4 vols.), 1974.

grief then arrives at the important conclusion that his experience of how God works has changed. The psalmist ardently prays:

> I cry aloud to God,
> cry aloud to God that he may hear me.
>
> In the day of my distress I sought the Lord.
> My hands were raised at night without ceasing;
> my soul refused to be consoled.
> I remembered my God and I groaned.
> I pondered and my spirit fainted.
>
> You withheld sleep from my eyes.
> I was troubled, I could not speak.
> I thought of the days long ago
> and remembered the years long past.
> At night I mused within my heart.
> I pondered and my spirit questioned.
>
> "Will the Lord reject us forever?
> Will he show us his favor no more?
> Has his love vanished for ever?
> Has his promise come to an end?
> Does God forget his mercy
> or in anger withhold his compassion"?
>
> I said: "This is what causes my grief:
> that the way of the Most High has changed."

When a priest experiences the pain of rejection or even hostility from the very people he has been trying to serve heroically, great anger and resentment can arise when he experiences the paschal death of the idealized notion he has had of himself as a priest or the idealized notion he has carried about the nature of a parish community. The priest can give prayerful expression to that anger and resentment when he recites in Psalm 35:22-23 (Thursday Morning Prayer, Week 1):

> O Lord, plead my cause against my foes;
> fight those who fight me.
> Take up your buckler and shield;
> arise to help me.

The important thing for a priest to recognize at this time in his life is that he cannot avoid the paschal death he must endure. Furthermore, he cannot conclude that this experience of desolation is a sign that God is absent or that his spiritual endeavors up to this point in his life have been a sham. In his *Spiritual Exercises*, St. Ignatius of Loyola offers some wonderful advice on how to negotiate such experiences of desolation. In the First Week of the Exercises, Ignatius offers "Rules for the Discernment of Spirits"; there are fourteen of them.[14] In rule 7, Ignatius describes desolation as the experience of God withdrawing from us "his abundant fervor, augmented love, and intensive grace, [though] he still supplies sufficient grace for our salvation."[15] Ignatius cautions that when we experience desolation we need to resist the tempting thought that God has abandoned us and instead purposefully consider how God is helping us through the desolation "even if we do not clearly perceive it."[16]

In commenting on this seventh rule of discernment of spirits, Timothy Gallagher teaches:

> Spiritual desolation, when it appears as purely futile process, is especially difficult to bear, and those who undergo it will all the more easily fall prey to its harmful promptings. Through the *consideration* Ignatius proposes, such persons cross the threshold *out* of this spontaneous sense of heavy meaninglessness and *into* awareness that there is, in fact, a God-intended meaning in their experience of desolation.[17]

Gallagher also notes the importance of working through the experiences of desolation and seeing them as threshold moments of growth, not merely as the painful loss of what had been very tangible experiences of consolation.

> When humbly and courageously resisted, spiritual desolation becomes, indeed, a crucial spiritual lesson, teaching hope and

---

14. St. Ignatius of Loyola, *The Spiritual Exercises of St. Ignatius of Loyola*, trans. George E. Ganss (St. Louis: The Institute of Jesuit Sources, 1992), 121–25.

15. Ibid., 123.

16. Ibid.

17. Timothy M. Gallagher, *The Discernment of Spirits: An Ignatian Guide for Everyday Living* (New York: Crossroad Publishing, 2005), 95.

guiding the person toward spiritual maturity in ways that spiritual consolation alone could not accomplish. . . . God's loving providence does not include only "half" of our experience—spiritual consolation, yes, spiritual desolation, no—but rather is *always* active in our lives, both in giving spiritual consolation and in permitting us to experience the trial of spiritual desolation. When spiritual consolation is embraced and spiritual desolation resisted, each movement permits its own kind of growth. *Both* are necessary, in the measure God's loving wisdom disposes, and both are, as Ignatius tells us, lessons. Through both, we come to "the full stature of Christ" (Eph 4:13).[18]

What is important to note in this paschal process is that one's grief cannot become regret or rejection of the Hero image that was so energizing at one time. While it may no longer dominate as a compelling image, it is important to note that for the priest at this stage to resist and endure the trials of desolation he will need to draw precisely from the archetypal energy of the Hero that brings forth persistence and fortitude. Therefore, the archetype of the "Hero-priest for Christ" ought to be regarded as a blessing and a wonderful period of tremendous grace from the Lord. Without this acceptance of the Hero's blessing, a man may erroneously conclude that he became a priest for all the wrong reasons and now must depart from ordained ministry. Furthermore, the period of true grief will reveal that the previously acknowledged operative motives for wanting to give one's life for Christ and his church and the pivotal underlying operative motives (which may not have been acknowledged up to that point) are no longer leading to the sense of success and satisfaction they once did; consolation has dissipated. Those motives too ought to be regarded as blessings, however, because they carried the man through all the years that have now led to this pivotal point in his life and in priesthood. Even though a priest will need to let go of some of his previous operative motives, he needs to see them as how the Spirit operated within him in his foundational period of discerning his priestly vocation and then initially living out his priestly life. As St. Thomas Aquinas reminds us, "Grace builds on nature."

18. Ibid., 99–100. How one works through the experience of desolation will be treated more fully in the next chapter.

Therefore, the motives that were a part of a man's inner life at an earlier stage of psychological and spiritual development (whether consciously or unconsciously) can be regarded as avenues of grace, even if those motives do not fully apply any longer.

Andre Papineau captures well the simultaneous experience of continuity and discontinuity that occurs within these liminal, paschal moments of developmental change. This kind of change does not, however, happen smoothly or easily. Papineau writes:

> Developmental changes in the adult life cycle . . . [involve] the breaking up or death of one world and the birth of another in relation to self and others. It implies losing ourselves and others in one way and finding them in a new way. Transitions generate a tension between a side of the self that needs to break with the status quo and a side that feels obligated to defend it because it is still identified with it. This tension is best described in the statement, "I am not what I was but I am not *not* what I was either."[19]

Both Papineau and Rolheiser make it clear that all liminal experiences in human growth and spiritual development will involve a painful "letting-go" of what once worked so well, an awkward "in-between" that lacks clarity of self-identity for a while, and then finally a "new beginning" with a new sense of self and inner spirit, but one that keeps elements of the old.

"Sublating" the Hero into a New Priestly Archetype

As painful and necessary as our paschal deaths may be, not everything that "dies" within them is lost forever. We certainly believe that while the flesh-bound incarnation of Christ died on Calvary, the personhood of Jesus did not end. In the resurrection, all that Jesus ever was and would forever be came to life again, but in a new way. Thus we can say that even in the discontinuity of his death, there was an underlying continuity of Christ's living personhood. His resurrected personal

---

19. Andre Papineau, *Breaking Up, Down, and Through: Discovering Spiritual and Psychological Opportunities in Your Transitions* (New York: Paulist Press, 1997), 12.

presence was no longer confined by time and space or human finitude; however, it was still the human and divine Jesus of Nazareth, but now Christ the risen Lord. He was fully alive in a manner that could never die again and in a way that was powerfully and universally life-giving to others. Likewise, the Hero within the priest does not fully die in the paschal death of his idealized version of being a noble man for Christ. Instead that heroic drive now takes on a new form, a new perspective on what it means to be a priest, and a new capacity to be that priest for Christ and for the church.

This process of conversion from one stage to another without the prior stage being totally lost is best understood vis-à-vis the process of "sublation," as proposed by Bernard Lonergan.[20] When delineating the forms of conversion that happen within a person (intellectual, moral, and religious), Lonergan describes the process as a constant course of further and deeper self-transcendence, in which the previous stages of thinking (intellectual), valuing (moral), and believing (religious) are drawn into the next stage.[21] For Lonergan, conversion happens on every level of human consciousness, so it is a psychological, emotional, intellectual, volitional, and spiritual process all at the same time. The dynamic of sublation is key to this integrated conversion because, as Lonergan states, each further stage of self-transcendence "introduces something new and distinct, puts everything on a new basis, yet so far from interfering with the [previous] sublated [stage] or destroying it, on the contrary needs it, includes it, preserves all its proper features and properties, and carries them forward to a fuller realization within a richer context."[22]

Since spiritual growth is essential to ongoing conversion, it is my contention that Lonergan's principle of sublation can also be used to explain how an earlier stage of spiritual development is lifted up into a later, more developed stage, without losing all the important features of the earlier stage. Or perhaps, rather than speaking of a spiritual sublation *up into a higher stage*, the better way of stating this is that

20. Bernard Lonergan, *Method in Theology* (Minneapolis, MN: Seabury Press, 1972), 241. The author credits Karl Rahner for the use of the term "sublation" in the manner in which it is applied in this text. Lonergan cites Rahner's *Hearer of the Word* (Munich: Kösel Publishing, 1963), 40.

21. Lonergan, *Method in Theology*, 241.

22. Ibid.

an earlier stage of spiritual growth at one level of human consciousness is sublated *down into a deeper level* of one's personhood without the graced features of the earlier stage being lost. The point here is that what the Holy Spirit accomplished within a man in the period of his initially fervent and dedicated desire to be a Noble Hero for Christ is not lost, even as that stage of spirituality falls apart. The paschal death of the Noble Hero does not annihilate the graced archetypal energy that rose within a priest for several years. Instead, that honorable and worthy energy must now become sublated by the Holy Spirit.

At this point, it is fitting to see the connection between how the Holy Spirit sublates one stage of archetypal energy into another and how the power of the Holy Spirit transforms bread and wine into the Body and Blood of Christ. Since the Eucharist is a vital part of priestly spirituality, seeing the connection between the ongoing conversion of a priest and the conversion of bread and wine into the real presence of Christ is important. To understand this, let us look at the writing of Michael Stebbins.

Stebbins, a gifted commentator on Lonergan's work, notes that for Lonergan a lower-order reality can be taken up into a higher-order reality without the destruction of the lower-order thing. The lower-order reality, however, can no longer be identified or named as what it once was; it has become sublated into the higher-order thing without being annihilated. Stebbins cites the example of oxygen within a molecule of a blood cell to demonstrate this phenomenon. He explains:

> To illustrate my point, a free molecule of oxygen is a thing; but oxygen bonded to a molecule of hemoglobin in one of my red blood cells is no longer a thing, since it is now functioning within a higher-order unity, identity, whole. At the same time, however, the oxygen is no less oxygen; . . . the conjugates or properties of oxygen remain unchanged, even though they are predicated of a higher-order thing. Lonergan refers to this kind of change as "sublation," by which he means that the reality of a lower-order thing is incorporated into the reality of a higher-order thing.[23]

23. J. Michael Stebbins, "The Eucharistic Presence of Christ: Mystery and Meaning," *Worship* 64 (1990): 225–36.

Stebbins goes on to apply this concept of sublation to the process of eucharistic conversion (most often referred to as "transubstantiation") whereby the lower-order realities of bread and wine are completely transformed into the higher-order realities of the Body and Blood of Christ without losing any of their qualities and characteristics as bread and wine.[24] This is done by the power of the Holy Spirit.

Notably, it is the same power of the Holy Spirit to effect the eucharistic conversion (transubstantiation) of bread and wine that brings about deeper conversion within every human person, including a priest. Through sublation, the Holy Spirit transforms a priest enduring a paschal death into a newly constituted priest—a man who lives and ministers out of the underlying current of a paschal intimacy with Christ. What this means is that the priest, who for so long has been dutifully invoking the epiclesis of the Holy Spirit in the eucharistic prayer for the sublation of bread and wine into the Body and Blood of Christ, ought always to pray for an epiclesis of his inner life so that the Holy Spirit can raise up all that he has been as a Noble Hero *for* Christ into the higher and deeper reality of priesthood whereby he now sees himself and becomes a Faithful Servant *with* Christ. This is the Pentecost moment in the paschal process,[25] whereby a faithful man can emerge from the paschal death of how he once saw himself as a priest and how he had once engaged in ministry for the church and let the Spirit of the new life come rushing into him so that he can now live the resurrected sense of priesthood to which God has led him. This Pentecost experience ushers in the next chapter in a priest's spiritual biography.

24. Stebbins contends that the eucharistic elements can no longer be identified as bread and wine, for they have ontologically and intelligibly become something infinitely more as the Real Presence of Christ. But they never lose anything of the experiential qualities and characteristics of bread and wine; they still look, taste, smell, and have the texture of bread and wine. This is how Christ's Body and Blood become sacred food and drink for all of us. Ibid., 228–30.

25. Rolheiser describes well this Pentecost moment; cf., *The Holy Longing*, 147.

✛ CHAPTER TWO

A Faithful Servant *with* Christ

And when [Jesus] got into the boat, his disciples followed him.
A windstorm arose on the sea, so great that the boat was
being swamped by the waves; but he was asleep. And they
went and woke him up, saying, "Lord, save us! We are perish-
ing!" And he said to them, "Why are you afraid, you of little
faith?" Then he got up and rebuked the winds and the sea;
and there was a dead calm. They were amazed, saying, "What
sort of man is this, that even the winds and the sea obey him?"
—Matthew 8:23-27

Emerging from the Hero's Death

Every priest eventually gets caught in a raging storm, whether it comes from the outer difficulties in ministry or the inner world of disappointment, loneliness, anger, or doubt. This is when the "ego self" at the core of the Hero needs to connect with Christ in a newer way to navigate what have become turbulent waters. The "ego self" is increasingly termed the "false self" by writers who have traced the contours of spiritual growth and development. One of the most insightful mentors who offers guidance through the necessary stages of the spiritual life is the well-known Franciscan priest Richard Rohr. In his wonderful text *Immortal Diamond: The Search for Our True Self*, Rohr describes early on the right way to understand the "false self" and then the necessary death it must undergo. He writes:

> Your False Self is not your bad self, your clever or inherently
> deceitful self, the self that God does not like or you should not

like. Actually your False Self is quite good and necessary as far as it goes. It just does not go far enough, and it often poses and thus substitutes for the real thing. That is its only problem, and that is why we call it "false." The False Self is bogus more than bad, and bogus only when it pretends to be more than it is. Various false selves (temporary costumes) are necessary to get us all started, and they show their limitations when they are around too long. If a person keeps growing, his or her various false selves usually die in exposure to greater light. . . . When you are able to move beyond your False Self—at the right time and in the right way—it *will feel precisely as if you have lost nothing.*[1]

Rohr's insistence that we not regard the false self as a bad self is very important for letting the "Noble Hero *for* Christ" stage of priesthood continue to grace a priest's life even after that stage has come to an end, often a painful and disconcerting end. As mentioned in the previous chapter, its "paschal death" does not indicate that the earlier stage was a misguided or erroneous step in the pathway of priesthood. Therefore, regret or self-incrimination about one's ability to properly discern the call of Christ cannot be allowed to take over a man's spirit. Instead, a man needs to see the paschal process he is enduring as true intimacy with Christ in his own paschal death and resurrection. This insight will hopefully lead to the awareness in the priest that Christ, who had heretofore been the nobly heroic "Other" standing in front of him as the icon of whom the priest himself was supposed to be, is now revealed as the intimate Companion, standing alongside the man in his prayer and ministry, seeking to be yoked to him in a priesthood of faithful service and self-giving.

This is what paschal deaths do—they yoke us to Christ in a way that is intimate, nourishing, and sustaining. In his wonderful book of reflections on his own paschal deaths and his impending death from cancer, Cardinal Joseph Bernardin captures well how anguish and pain

---

1. Richard Rohr, *Immortal Diamond: The Search for Our True Self* (San Francisco: Jossey-Bass, 2013), 27–28. This insightful book by Rohr is actually the third in a series. The first text is *The Naked Now: Learning to See as the Mystics See* (New York: Crossroads, 2009). The second text is the one cited in the previous chapter, *Falling Upward: A Spirituality of the Two Halves of Life* (San Francisco: Jossey-Bass, 2011).

can be redemptive and transformative if we recognize how in them we have become true companions of Christ. In pondering the important words of Jesus in Matthew 11:28-30 in which the Lord invites us to come to him, find rest in him, and take his yoke upon our shoulders, Bernardin writes:

> What does Jesus mean by his "yoke"? The ancient rabbis used to refer to the Mosaic Law as a kind of yoke. But Jesus' metaphor is different because central to his "yoke" or wisdom or law is the Lord himself. . . . Usually a yoke joined a pair of oxen and made them a team. It is as though Jesus tells us, "Walk alongside me; learn to carry the burdens by observing how I do it. If you let me help you, the heavy labor will seem lighter."[2]

Once the Hero recognizes that he is not all that he thought he was as a priest and that he will not accomplish all that he thought he would in priesthood (or in a particular ministry or assignment in priesthood), the Hero archetype can be yoked to Christ in a new way in priesthood and enter into the "Faithful Servant *with* Christ" stage.[3]

This constitutes a genuine refoundation of one's sense of vocation to priestly life and ministry and most likely also a man's sense of self-identity as the False Self now lends itself to the discovery of the True Self. As this refoundation work begins, however, the previous archetypal energy of the Hero is still needed because the man needs to find within him the valiant capacity to stay the course even though he is feeling lost, empty, lonely, disappointed, perhaps somewhat fearful, possibly even angry at God for the unravelling of what once sustained him. This is when heroic courage begins to be lived in a different manner.

St. Thomas Aquinas called courage one of the four cardinal virtues, yet he goes on to note that it is manifested in different ways in different

---

2. Joseph Bernardin, *The Gift of Peace* (Chicago: Loyola Press, 1997), 124–26.

3. Admittedly, some seminarians or newly ordained priests may be found in this stage early on. They may exhibit an already well-honed capacity to journey alongside people in their needs. If the man has not previously undergone some appropriation of the Hero archetype within him, he will need to discover how to summon the energy of the Hero in order to push through the moments when his efforts at being the Servant are opposed, dismissed, or unsuccessful in achieving the end for which he was hoping.

circumstances or stages of life. In his *Summa Theologica*, Aquinas speaks of courage as the capacity and strength for "standing one's ground amidst dangers," especially those dangers that threaten bodily harm and death.[4] In the initial expression of this courage, a priest has utter confidence in what God and he can do together, perhaps with the help of others.[5] But later on or in different circumstances, Aquinas notes that the courageous person will demonstrate a noble patience and perseverance. This is a quieter form of the same cardinal virtue seen when the Hero meets the brokenness of life; only now the priest does not become discouraged or undone by sorrow, disappointment, or the painful recognition of his own limitations.[6] He endures with magnanimity the difficulties of priestly life. With this kind of courage, the priest perseveres in ministry but discovers a new form of strength, one that is recognized as a gift of Christ's Spirit offered to each faithful companion of Christ in ministry. This is when the paschal death of the Hero, who has undergone a resurrection into a new life of being yoked to Christ as a Servant, now experiences the Pentecost that Christ promises.

From Paschal Death to Pentecost Courage

We ought to become comfortable speaking not of a singular Pentecost but of Pentecosts. The first moment of Pentecost did not give the followers of Christ a once-and-for-all understanding of all they were to be and to do in their mission for Christ or a once-and-for-all boost of courage to sustain them in that mission. In the Acts of the Apostles, Luke refers to a series of various kinds of Pentecosts. There is the foundational and explicitly named event of Pentecost in Jerusalem where the Spirit drives the disciples out of their fear in the Upper Room and out into the streets to boldly proclaim Christ (Acts 2:1-42). Also in Jerusalem, however, after Peter and John are arrested and the persecution of the early Christians begins, the community of disciples prays for boldness and courage, and once again the room shakes and all are filled with the Holy Spirit (Acts 4:23-31).

---

4. Thomas Aquinas, "Courage," vol. 42 of *Summa Theologica*, trans. Blackfriars (New York: McGraw-Hill, 1966), IIa, IIae, 123.6.

5. Ibid., *ST*, IIa, IIae, 129.6.

6. Ibid., *ST*, IIa, IIae, 128.1.

The series of Pentecosts continues when the Way of Christ moves beyond the confines of Jerusalem. Philip heads to Samaria and proclaims the Gospel and baptizes many believers. Later, Peter and John join him and lay their hands on the newly baptized who then receive the Holy Spirit (Acts 8:1-17). As the nascent church moves further north into the Gentile world, another Pentecost occurs in Caesarea, where the Holy Spirit descends on the uncircumcised while Peter is addressing them (Acts 10:34-48). Finally, as the Gospel reaches Ephesus in Asia Minor, Pentecost again happens when Paul baptizes twelve disciples and lays hands upon them, whereupon they receive the Holy Spirit, speak in tongues, and prophesy (Acts 19:1-7).

In all of these Pentecosts, the Holy Spirit moves the apostles to the next moment of growth and development: (1) from being fearful/hidden disciples to becoming bold and public witnesses; (2) from cowering under the threat of persecution to proclaiming Christ as free and faithful witnesses; (3) from being in a single location in Jerusalem to moving to a new location in Samaria; (4) from existing solely in the Jewish world to embracing the world of the Gentiles; (5) from being contained only in the land of Jesus to bursting into the land of Greece and eventually the land of Rome.

What is important for us to realize is that, since "Pentecosts" is plural, we can be confident that the Holy Spirit is animating every single new moment in our own journeys of faith and our own fulfillment of the priestly mission in which we have been ordained. This allows us to recognize that when "what has been" is no longer working, this does not mean that the Spirit we received at ordination has abandoned us. It means that the Holy Spirit is leading us to the new "what could be" in our inner lives, in our operative motives for priesthood, and in the manner in which we live out our lives and ministry as priests with courage and hope. Therefore, the Spirit moves us to the next moment of our own spiritual growth and development: (1) from being afraid of acknowledging our own limitations, perhaps even hiding them, to openly admitting them to God, ourselves, and perhaps a spiritual director; (2) from being too constricted in our self-knowledge about some of our underlying, operative motives to admitting them freely and letting God claim them; (3) from being mired in one place in our spiritual journey to going to a new and deeper place; (4) from seeing priesthood solely from the perspective that we have always known and that has been very comfortable and affirming to us to now seeing priesthood in a more complex manner but one that allows more co-operation with what Christ needs from us; (5) and, finally, from living in only one world of meaning for ministry, one theological perspective, one worldview, to breaking out of our secure niches to be with Christ in different worlds of meaning, with different theological perspectives, and with different priorities for living out priesthood.

As with the apostles, these new Pentecosts will not always be easy. They will come only with leaving behind old comforts and old fears. They will push us into a new level of awareness of how the Holy Spirit is operative inside of us and all around us in ways previously not known to us. Furthermore, as in the Acts of the Apostles, each Pentecost will demand that we move out of some hidden room inside of us, out of some comfortable place that has housed all of our unexamined motives and conclusions regarding priesthood, and out of some of our ways of operating and dealing with others to embrace what is new, different, wider, larger, and most assuredly deeper in the spiritual life and the exercise of priesthood.

Since "Pentecosts" is plural, the Spirit-event will happen over and over again, but always at the end of another paschal process in our lives. Therefore, each "en-Spirited" moment of new life, after perhaps months or years of graced energy and sustenance, will eventually lead to another paschal death. This is to say that each Pentecost comes after the end of a death and resurrection in our spiritual and ministerial lives, but then it eventually leads to a further paschal death and resurrection down the road. The repeated nature of the paschal process in which the Holy Spirit is often trying to lead us to a new Pentecost means that we will always need to rely on our spiritual connection to Christ to navigate successfully the waters of rebirth into which we are being pulled, for it is Christ who bestows his Spirit on us.

These new Pentecosts can elude so many priests when they stay hidden in their upper rooms of security, safety, and fear of letting go of "what has been." This is when a priest remains stuck in an earlier stage of the spiritual life that his priesthood needs to move beyond because, as with the Pentecosts that moved the church to new places and different ways of being church in the Acts of the Apostles, our priesthood always has to move to new and different places of development and growth. In addition, the resistance to a new Pentecost happens when a priest becomes imprisoned in his own anger, disappointment, doubt, resentment, and perhaps rationalizations that have been fueling compensatory behaviors in his life. Furthermore, if a priest has not learned how to go deeper in prayer, if the inner life has always seemed daunting and dangerous, then he does not have any awareness that it is actually the Holy Spirit who is trying to unravel some of "what has been" in a priest's self-awareness, sense of vocation, and vision of priesthood and church. The Spirit had to do this with Simon Peter; the Spirit had to do this with St. Paul; the Spirit has to do this with us.

Our spiritual journey as priests cannot be a series of "Pentecosts lost" but needs to embrace the continued paschal process in our lives that will always lead to new descents of the Holy Spirit on us. If we allow ourselves to go deeper into the spiritual life, to recognize and then mourn our paschal deaths, to look for resurrections, to enter our upper rooms of prayer and reflection and discernment, to open up to the Holy Spirit, then we will emerge from "what has been" to live out the spirit of "what now is" in our priestly life and ministry. Over time, the Pentecosts of priesthood will allow us to surrender more fully everything that God claimed about our identity, our personhood, our archetypal energies on the day we were ordained.

The Ontological Claim *by the Holy Spirit*

It is the Holy Spirit who configures us to the priesthood of Christ and seeks to bring about an essential and permanent oneness with Jesus the Eternal Priest. But while our priesthood is the priesthood of Jesus Christ, the Son of God, it is also the priesthood of the same Christ who became incarnate in order to touch, embrace, and heal every aspect of human brokenness. Therefore, the Holy Spirit, by configuring us to the Incarnate Priest, claims everything about our humanness, including all that is broken about us as persons and as priests. This is where there is a need perhaps to adjust some of our theological thinking in order to gain better spiritual insight. Since the Middle Ages, influenced by the earlier writings of St. Augustine, the church has taught that baptism, confirmation, and holy orders are unrepeatable sacraments because they affect us on the level of our being. Very often, therefore, being ordained a priest was described by the church as an "ontological change"; and so it is. But that kind of language all by itself without a wider sacramental context has proven to be problematic. In some cases it has led to clerical elitism and entitlement. In other cases it has led to ministerial malpractice and a lack of accountability because some priests mistakenly assume that no matter how well or how poorly they perform their duties all will be satisfactory priestly ministry. And in some cases it has led to walking away from priesthood because a man might never have experienced the benefits of ontological change in times of great loneliness or struggle.

Because of these misconceptions, I prefer to speak less about *ontological change* and more about *ontological claim*. By this I mean that at our ordination the Holy Spirit claimed us for the Priesthood of Jesus Christ at the very core of our being, but the experiential effects of that claim will take the rest of our lives to unfold. Think of it: each of us at ordination lay on the floor of a cathedral or church in an act of complete surrender to Christ. Then we knelt before the bishop in a humble posture of self-giving and of complete receptivity to the outpouring of the Holy Spirit. But when we rose from that floor and stood as priest (and, beforehand, as a deacon), were we different persons? Well, yes and no. Yes, we were, at the core of our being, more configured to Christ the Priest. But, in other ways we were not any different than we once were. On the levels of our personality, our attitudes and dispositions, our ways of thinking and feeling and desiring—on all of these levels, we were pretty much the person we had always been. We did not stop being ourselves. Our personal histories remained intact. Our struggles and joys, our loves and losses remained inside of us. Our abilities and limitations still held. But the Holy Spirit was not done with us. Slowly over time our inner unity with Christ, effected by the Holy Spirit, has been working its way through our personal identity and transforming the very broken, limited, and flawed ways that we have lived out priesthood and experienced priestly life. And the Spirit claims all of that.

To be sure, the theological notion of the ontological change in a man who is ordained has tremendous value when it reminds us that priesthood (and diaconate as well) is not a mere function, job, or career; nor is it the expression of only a temporary commitment to Christ and his church in a man's life. It is the manner in which the Holy Spirit unites a man's essence, personhood, and way of life to the identity of

Christ as Priest on behalf of the church and the world. The experiential effects of this ontological change happen slowly over time, however, as the Holy Spirit draws the priest into one Pentecost after another after another.

When I was on retreat several years ago, while I was experiencing a rather painful paschal process in priestly life and I was long past feeling heroic and I was not sensing very tangibly the companionship of Christ, the following poem came to me as a result of very difficult days in prayer. I have titled the poem "Surrender."

> The rock sits
> at the shore of the sea—
> solid,
> confident,
> defiant . . .
>
> . . . while the sea laps
> over the rock—
> gracious,
> welcoming,
> constant.
>
> The rock does not seem to move,
> to give.
> But slowly
> one infinitely small particle after another
> is set free
> into the water's current.
>
> And the rock becomes the sea.

It seems that the deeper waters of the spiritual life are not only a forceful stream of grace that we need to learn to navigate well; they are also a powerful but gentle current that keeps drawing us in, bit by bit, moment by moment, through one paschal process after another. Because it is God who is always doing this at our deepest core—our ontological center of being—God will constantly seek to draw us into the deeper waters. As with our baptism, each plunge into the water brings a new infusion of the Spirit, a new Pentecost. While the

Pentecosts of Scripture happened with a dramatic flair, the Pentecosts of our lives, in which we are claimed more and more by the Holy Spirit, can often happen subtly, slowly, almost surreptitiously. But they *do* happen for each priest who stays committed to the work of the interior life of prayer. The manner in which Pentecost unfolds for one priest, however, may not be the same for another. Pentecosts happen uniquely within each priest's particular experience of being claimed by the Holy Spirit for intimacy with Christ the Priest.

Praying and Serving with Christ

John Duns Scotus, the thirteenth-century Franciscan philosopher, captured well an important theological principle that can be aptly applied to the spiritual life; it is the notion of *haecceitas*, which recognizes that the sacred is encountered in the particularity or "thisness" of our experiences.[7] In Richard Rohr's use of Scotus's principle, God did not create generic forms of being "but only specific and unique incarnations of the Eternal Mystery—each one chosen, loved, and preserved in existence as itself—*by being itself.*"[8] The notion of *haecceitas* invites us to discover our intimacy with Christ in the particularities of our lives. This manner of spiritual exercise allows us to cry out in certain belief, "Christ is with me in *this* experience." We can assert with confidence, "Christ is here with me in *this* painful or unsettling or difficult time in my life." In short, Christ is our Companion in *this* moment, whatever *this* moment may be.

The power behind the kind of insight gained from applying *haecceitas* to our spiritual journey happens when we gain a deeply personal feeling of connectedness to the concreteness of Jesus' life and ministry. More often than not, general intellectual notions of the paschal mystery or redemptive suffering do not aid a person in the midst of gut-level painful or confusing experiences. Likewise, pious concepts about the need to go deeper in prayer or the importance of surrendering more fully to God do not captivate a troubled spirit that feels drained of joy or consolation. What is needed is a heartfelt encounter with the

---

7. See Scotus's *Early Oxford Lecture on Individuation*, trans. Allan B. Wolter (St. Bonaventure, NY: Franciscan Institute, 2005), esp. 81–85.

8. Rohr, *Immortal Diamond*, 18.

person of Jesus Christ whose own particular experiences resonate with what we are going through in the "this-ness" of our lives.

For me, the Ignatian style of imaginative prayer has proven very fruitful in fostering valuable heartfelt connections between the "this-ness" of Christ and my own. By allowing the Holy Spirit to engage one's imagination in Ignatian prayer, the pray-er then enters a scene from Jesus' public life and ministry or from Jesus' hidden life (all of those moments in Jesus' earthly existence not recounted in Scripture).[9] When encountering Jesus in this manner of prayer, the pray-er then lets Jesus' own heart, mind, and inner life be revealed in a personal way. Because we believe that in the incarnation Jesus is truly human, with a real human mind, heart, body, soul, and inner life, then we can be assured that he has taken into himself all human experiences. Besides experiencing true human joy, love, laughter, gratitude, hope, enthusiasm, zeal, and deep commitment, Jesus also knows human anguish, frustration, loneliness, sadness, disappointment, failure, grief, and struggle. Nothing of our particular experiences as human beings and as ordained priests is disconnected from the particular experiences of Jesus of Nazareth. Nothing about the unsettling paschal process in which we feel an acute "dislocation" from what was once a fulfilling spiritual life and priestly existence to an unsure sense of who and where we need to be in our lives is out of range of Jesus' own struggles to discover over and over again where the Father is leading him and what the Father asks of him.

At this juncture in a priest's spiritual life and self-understanding, it is important to see what is unfolding—a shift from primarily being a priest *for* Christ to instead experiencing how one is a priest and servant *with* Christ. Looking at the gospels, we find many particular moments in Jesus' life and ministry that invite us to discover in countless ways how he (or any other major gospel figure closely connected to Jesus) is a true companion in every particular dimension of our priestly life and ministry. Below is a brief outline of an Ignatian method of prayerfully engaging Christ in the intimate connectedness he offers to all aspects of our lives as ordained ministers:

9. At the end of John's gospel we read: "But there are also many other things that Jesus did; if every one of them were written down, I suppose that the world itself could not contain the books that would be written" (John 21:25).

1. Spend a few moments in solitude becoming aware of what has been stirring inside of you that you need to bring to Christ in your prayer.

2. Ask the Holy Spirit to lead you in your prayer and name specifically the grace for which you are asking. Invite the saints who mean something to you to be by your side as you engage in this prayer.

3. Read the relevant Scripture passage slowly. If praying over a moment in the hidden life of Jesus, begin to imagine the scene.

4. Let the Holy Spirit lead your imagination into the scene more fully as you observe and listen to what is unfolding in the scene.

5. Become aware of where Jesus is in relation to you in this scene. If praying with a figure other than Jesus but who is closely connected to Jesus (e.g., Mary, Joseph, or John the Baptist), then imagine where that figure is in relation to you.

6. Become aware of what you are hearing and noticing and also what begins to stir inside of you.

7. If the scene involves Jesus, wait to discover what he is trying to say or do or offer you in the moment. If the scene involves a different biblical figure, wait to discover what that figure is trying to say or do or offer you.

8. After the scene begins to fade from your imaginative prayer, recite an Our Father or other favorite prayers.

9. Then capture in a journal the insights you gained from the prayer, including the most subtle hints of a grace that unfolded or the most obvious forms of resistance or distraction that arose within you during the prayer.

10. If nothing really happened in the prayer, then return to it later in the day, if possible, or the next day. Trust that Christ desires to be with you in an intimate way in your prayer and in whatever you are experiencing.

Because the spiritual life of any person, including a priest, does not happen in a generic unfolding of life but arises out of the concrete and specific circumstances one experiences, this form of Ignatian prayer is particularly helpful when someone is searching for meaning in the midst of difficult moments. It is also helpful for those seeking consolation and courage when the particular situations of ministry have led to disappointment or desolation. These kinds of experiences, which can feel overwhelmingly empty and isolating, need a sense of connection to Christ. They need the intimacy of being with Christ who knows well what one is experiencing deep inside and, therefore, is a very real companion in what one is enduring. Therefore, one's prayer at this point needs to discover key points of intersection between the *haecceitas* of Christ and one's own. What follows is a list of possible points of intersection that can happen in a priest's prayer. The list is in no way meant to be exhaustive of the range of experiences in which a priest needs to find Christ's companionship, nor is it intentionally exclusive of other passages that might be more helpful in prayer.

1. **Dealing with failure:**
   It is clear, especially in the Synoptic gospels, that the disciples more often than not do not grasp what Jesus is teaching. See Mark 8:31-33; Mark 9:30-32; Mark 10:32-37.

2. **Having to change course/plans:**
   The infancy narratives are filled with moments when Joseph and Mary had to deal with very unexpected circumstances demanding a change of course in their lives. See Matthew 1:18-25; 2:13-17; 2:19-23.

   Jesus had to adjust his plans when circumstances demanded. See Mark 1:40-45; Matthew 15:21-28; Luke 15:21-28; or John 4:1-3.

3. **Experiencing loneliness:**
   Certainly in his hidden life there were many moments when Jesus realized that those around him could never truly understand him or be completely fulfilling companions.

   The pivotal moments for Jesus' sense of loneliness in his public life come in the passion narratives. See Mark 14:43-50 and 15:33-34.

4. **Facing rejection:**
   Both Jesus' hometown of Nazareth and the city of Jerusalem ultimately cannot accept him. See Matthew 13:54-58; Luke 4:16-30; and 13:34-35.

Jesus invites the rich young man to follow him, but the man walks away. See Mark 10:17-22. (Notice that Jesus looks upon the man with love, making the man's rejection even more acute for Jesus.)

After his amazing claims in the Bread of Life discourse, many in the crowd who once followed Jesus walk away from him. See John 6:60-66.

The crowd in Jerusalem prefers Barabbas over Jesus. See Matthew 27:15-26 or Luke 23:13-25.

5. **Enduring betrayal and denial by close companions:**
Peter and Judas represent all those to whom we have looked for friendship and support but who end up, even for a crucial moment, turning away from us or even against us. See Luke 22:54-62 (Peter is right next to Jesus when he denies him) and John 13:21-30 (Jesus knows what Judas is about to do when they break bread together).

All four gospels recount the moment of betrayal by Judas. See Mark 14:43-46; Matthew 26:47-50; Luke 22:47-48; and John 18:1-13.

6. **Discerning whom to call forth as co-workers in pastoral leadership and ministry:**
Jesus often withdraws into prayer and solitude before calling disciples or calling forth the apostles from the midst of the disciples. See Matthew 4:12-22 and Luke 6:12-16.

7. **Needing to be alone:**
Jesus often felt the need to pull away from his public ministry and be in solitude. See Mark 1:32-35; Matthew 14:14-23; or Luke 4:40-42.

8. **Experiencing grief and despair:**
In the hidden life of Jesus, he had to deal with the death of Joseph.

In his public ministry, Jesus paused to grieve the death of John the Baptist and his friend Lazarus. See Matthew 14:9-13 and John 11:33-35.

Jesus is filled with sadness over Jerusalem's impending fate. See Luke 19:41-44.

9. **Being unsettled in life:**
   Jesus does not have a home and family as other people do and
   never gets to stay in one place for too long. See Matthew 8:18-22;
   12:46-50; and Mark 3:31-35.

10. **Facing conflict and tension while seeking to establish com-
    munion:**
    Jesus dines with Simon the Pharisee but also welcomes a sinful
    woman to the table. See Luke 7:36-50.

    Jesus faces the harshness of the Pharisees but creates a space for
    mercy for the adulterous woman. See John 8:1-11.

11. **Rejecting the False Self and discovering one's True Self:**
    Jesus faces down the temptations to become someone he is not
    meant to be and disallows false notions of who he is as the Mes-
    siah. See Matthew 4:1-11 or Luke 4:1-13 as well as Matthew
    16:13-23 and Luke 22:24-27.

    Jesus comes to know who he truly is in relationship to the Father
    and who he is for the world. See Mark 1:9-11; Luke 2:41-52;
    Matthew 12:15-21.

12. **Embracing celibacy:**
    In his hidden life, Jesus must have come to the recognition that
    he was to defy cultural norms and remain unmarried so as to
    devote his life completely to his mission.

    At the same time, during the years before he emerged on the
    public scene, Jesus must have come to the heartfelt experience
    that the Father's love for him was enough, perhaps from praying
    over and over again Psalm 63.

    Some parables of Jesus reveal his inner experience of being
    claimed fully by the kingdom of God within him. See especially
    Matthew 13:44-46.

13. **Dealing with turmoil:**
    Jesus calms the storms and settles the turbulence that has arisen
    around the disciples. See Matthew 8:23-27 or Mark 4:35-41.

    Jesus comes to the disciples as their boat is being battered by the
    waves. He invites Simon Peter to walk on the water and stay
    above the turmoil with him. See Matthew 14:22-33.

14. **Wanting to avoid a painful experience that lies ahead:**
    Jesus prays, "My Father, if it is possible, let this cup pass from me," yet he discovers a deeper trust in the Father's will. See Matthew 26:38-46 or Mark 14:34-42.

    Even though Jesus experiences a tremendous inner passion before his public passion unfolds, he experiences being strengthened by God. See Luke 22:39-46.

With all of the above suggested Scripture passages, and others like them, the key to praying with them is to allow the Holy Spirit to join us to the inner life of Jesus, to which only the Spirit can give us access. The fruit of this kind of praying is the recognizable shift from wanting a prayer life that engenders the capacity to do things for Christ to now also desiring a prayer life that can ponder a particular experience with Christ so as to be attuned to Christ's mind and heart in order to be a priest with him. The whole reason for the incarnation of Christ is the desire of God to be with us, intimately, powerfully, and redemptively.

Matthew's gospel account of the incarnation provides a marvelous example of scriptural inclusion by beginning and ending on the same note. At the beginning of the gospel, an angel in a dream reveals to Joseph the identity of the child of Mary; he is Emmanuel, God-with-us (Matt 1:23). At the end of the gospel, when the risen Christ summons his disciples to Galilee, he appears to them on a mountaintop and commissions them as ministers to go out to the whole world preaching, teaching, and baptizing others into discipleship and the communion of the Trinity. Then Christ offers this powerful promise and reassurance to the Eleven: "And remember, I am with you always, to the end of the age" (Matt 28:20). It is Emmanuel who will accompany the disciples throughout their ministry.

In similar fashion, Mark ends his gospel with a great commissioning and then goes on to describe how after the ascension of Christ the disciples "went out and proclaimed the good news everywhere, while the Lord worked with them and confirmed the message by the signs that accompanied it" (Mark 16:20). Indeed we see the followers of Christ in the Acts of the Apostles performing many of the same signs as Jesus did in his public ministry: Peter and John heal a man who is lame (Acts 3:1-10); the apostles cure many who are sick (Acts 5:12-16); Stephen forgives those who are putting him to death (Acts 7:54-60); Philip expels unclean spirits (Acts 8:4-8); Peter raises the dead (Acts 9:36-43).

These scriptural accounts of the promise and confirmation that Christ will continue to be present to those who continue his ministry ought to buoy the spirits of priests as they discover the companionship of Christ in their prayer. At this point in one's spiritual biography, it is no longer enough to see priestly ministry solely as a noble enterprise of a man who desires to be a Hero for Christ because after a while that archetypal energy can sometimes feel like a very lonely pledge or seem like a fruitless venture. At this point in the spiritual life, instead of a priest seeing Christ ahead of him, beckoning him forward in his heroic ministry, the priest now experiences Christ tangibly at his side, being a servant with the priest in the sacred "this-ness" of the man's priestly life and ministry, with all of its very particular struggles and triumphs, disappointments and joys, conflicts and relationships.

The more that a priest can pray into the precise connections between the "this-ness" in Jesus' hidden or public life and his own experiences in *this* particular pastoral assignment, *this* parish, *this* group of people, *this* staff of people with whom he is working, *this* issue that is surfacing at *this* moment in a man's priesthood, *this* question or doubt or longing, then the more Christ truly becomes Emmanuel for him—God-with-him-in-his-priesthood. It is from that personal sense of the incarnate Christ-at-his-side that a priest's archetypal energy and courage shift from the yearning for valiant accomplishment to the longing for fidelity in service to God's People.

Even within this faithful energy, however, the tangibility of Christ's companionship will not always be vivid or obvious. It will often require returning over and over again to praying imaginatively with scenes of connectedness between Jesus' life and ministry and the priest's. One important tool for capturing the graces of prayer might be journal writing. With a journal, one can develop the habit of recording the sometimes intense and sometimes subtle insights of one's prayerful encounters with Christ. Journal entries can "hold" moments of recognizable experiences of Christ's companionship and invite the pray-er back into those moments weeks, months, even years later. In addition, these journal entries can remind the pray-er that even if he does not feel right now the palpability of Christ at his side, intense encounters with Christ have happened very really before and will happen again. In the meantime, these recorded prayer experiences can help to alleviate the priest's anxiousness that he is all alone in whatever difficulty he is going through and in what might be unfolding in the particular responsibilities and struggles of his priestly life and ministry; everything he is facing or enduring, he does so with Christ at his side—Emmanuel-with-him-in-his-priesthood. The heroic "I" of the earlier stage of priesthood now becomes a more persevering "We."

Priesthood Shifts from an "I" to a "We"

At the moments of both diaconate and priesthood ordinations, each of us who were to be ordained stood before the bishop and made solemn promises to be celibate, prayerful men who were willing to be more configured to Christ in service and in the sacred mysteries that we would celebrate. And then we knelt before the bishop and placed our hands within the bishop's and declared our pledge of humble obedience. During the ordination, the bishop asked us a series of questions, and each individual responded with great conviction "I am" (if we were ordained before the 1990s) or "I do" (if we were ordained since then). It was an important and significant thing for us to give our personal consent to what we were going to live and do as ordained deacons and then later priests. No one else could give that consent for us. No other "I" could speak those promises on our behalf. We were truly giving everything about our individuality over to the grace of God that claimed us from that day forward as ordained men for the church. Nevertheless, eventually the fervent and heroic assent of the "I" to be configured to Christ the true Deacon and Priest would have to collapse in order to be a sacred "We" with Christ. Furthermore, as most priests discover early on, the manner in which they are configured more fully to Christ happens as they immerse themselves into the life of the ecclesial community they serve. Thus, the forming of the sacred "We" with Christ occurs in and through ministry within the hallowed "We" of the church.

From the apostolic era onward, ministry was never meant to be the exercise of a solo agent, relying on his or her own abilities and internal resources to accomplish great things for Christ. At some point, all ministers in the church need to recognize that what we do and what we live are done with Christ and with one another as the church. Christ empowers our ministry with his Spirit. Christ is at work in our ministry through his Spirit. Christ draws us to his side in our ministry by his Spirit. And Christ's Spirit draws us to each other as co-workers with the Lord.

In the Johannine account of the death and resurrection of Christ, his desire for companionship with and among the disciples is made quite evident. For instance, hanging on the cross, Jesus unites his first disciple (his mother) and his beloved disciple to each other as they are united in devotion to Christ (John 19:25-27). On the night of the resurrection, the risen Christ bursts through the locked doors where the disciples are hiding and breathes his Spirit upon them, filling them with his gift of peace and then commissioning them to bring his forgiveness into the world (John 20:19-23). These scenes demonstrate that being empowered by the Holy Spirit and having devotion to Christ lead to an amazing oneness with Christ in ministry that is, at the same time, to become a strong impetus to foster communion with others in doing the work of the Lord.

That oneness with Christ is found, however, when those who minister do so in the manner and mind-set of Christ. In other words, to minister with Christ means to place ourselves where Christ is or, rather, to let Christ draw us to where he is. And where is Christ? The Last Supper accounts in both Luke's and John's gospels reveal the answer. After sharing the sacred meal with his disciples on the night before he dies, Jesus shares some important instructions with his followers on how they are to continue his mission after he is gone. In Luke's account, Jesus warns the disciples against the need for prominence and prestige as found among the political leaders of the Gentiles. Instead, as leaders the disciples of Jesus are to become servants. After all, Jesus asks, "who is greater, the one who is at table or the one who serves? Is it not the one at the table? But I am among you as one who serves" (see Luke 22:24-27). A priest will never experience a deep and sustaining oneness with Christ until he surrenders the ego's (the "I's") need for importance and achievement and discovers the freedom and power that come from true servanthood alongside of Christ.

The footwashing scene in John's Last Supper account makes this same point in an even more striking way. After clearly letting us know that Jesus is truly God,[10] the gospel writer then recounts the startling scene in which the Almighty One stoops down to take on the role of

---

10. John tells us that Jesus knows everything that is about to happen to him (13:1, 3) and that he has all power from God, had come from God, and was returning to God (13:3).

the household slave and wash the feet of the household guests, his disciples. The gesture is so disconcerting that Peter objects, not able to comprehend how his Master and Lord could perform such a lowly, servile task. Only after Peter consents to being served by Jesus can Jesus then invite his disciples into intimacy with him in that place of service. Rising up from washing their feet, Jesus announces, "For I have set you an example, that you also should do as I have done to you" (John 13:4-17).

As priests, we either perform or witness up close this footwashing—this *mandatum*—every Holy Thursday, on the very night we also celebrate Christ's institution of the priesthood. If we prayerfully engage this mandate from Christ, we will be renewed in the call to be one with our Mighty Savior in his lowliness and to discover the power of priesthood in the powerlessness of servanthood. If we let the *mandatum* draw us into honest self-reflection, we will discover that so much of what we struggle with internally as priests comes from our ego's resistance to embracing the self-emptying of Christ who is among us as one who serves, as one who stoops down to touch people where they are most vulnerable to the world's harshness and soiled by it.

In speaking about this iconic footwashing scene in the Upper Room, Pope Francis has said: "Washing one another's feet signifies welcoming, accepting, loving, and serving one another. It means serving the poor, the sick, and the outcast, those whom I find difficult, those who annoy me."[11] In order to adopt this level of self-giving, it would be good for priests to repeatedly return to these Last Supper scenes and through imaginative prayer ask Jesus to reveal how his own heart, mind, and spirit were able to forego heroic greatness to embrace lowly servanthood. This place of meeting Christ, who is among us as One who serves, is where the powerful archetypal energy of the Faithful Servant priest will arise. In this place of meeting, the "I am" or "I do" that we pledged for Christ at our ordinations becomes a "We are" or "We do" with Christ in fruitful and sustained years of priesthood.

---

11. Pope Francis, "Words from the Upper Room," in *I Ask You, Be Shepherds: Reflections on Pastoral Ministry*, trans. Michael O'Hearn (New York: Herder and Herder, 2015), 1.

Staying Faithful When Christ's Companionship Is Not Enough

Despite all the wonderful energy and inner freedom that can come from Christ's companionship, it can leave us wanting at times. Even when we stay faithful to the interior life, there will be moments of experiencing a distance from Christ, and sometimes the smallest space between ourselves and Christ-by-our-side can feel like a giant chasm. This chasm surfaces in different ways for different priests: the feelings of ineffectiveness that come from the lack of results after years of ministry, the lingering desires for intimacy that lead to lonely nights over and over again, the recurring regrets that invade one's attempts at solitude and prayer, the loss of loved ones that makes a priest wonder to whom he really does belong, the repeated frustrations with certain personalities and problems in the day-to-day exercise of priestly service, the slow descent of a malaise and disquietude on a priest's heart and spirit about vocation or prayer or even life in general. This chasm that develops between ourselves and Christ-by-our-side suggests that, after a while, no matter how much we pray, no matter how hard we work, no matter how faithful we are, all priests have to face and meet head on the incompleteness of their lives, even the insufficiency of priestly life to fulfill every desire within them. This is when a second level of desolation can set in; but, as stated earlier, God allows for the desolation in order to "bring us to full stature in Christ."

As part of this process of being brought to "full stature in Christ," even prayerful and dedicated priests will discover at some point that ministering side-by-side with Christ, no matter how spiritually and psychologically fulfilling it once was, is no longer enough. It *cannot* be enough because the desire of Christ is not merely genuine companionship with us but, even more so, a mutual indwelling of us in Christ and Christ in us. For that mutual indwelling to become operative archetypal energy, the current archetype of a priest as a Faithful Servant with Christ must undergo a paschal death and then a sublation to a higher spiritual state, as we saw with the earlier archetypal energy of the Noble Hero. All paschal deaths, however, as previously noted, come from a painful or unsettling desolation, even as they lead to a deeper grace.

This "second fathom of desolation," as I call it, is different from what was experienced during the paschal death of the Noble Hero for Christ. This new level of desolation comes less from what a priest discovers he cannot do or cannot be for Christ and for the church and more from a growing recognition that at his very core something is missing from his life—something that years of priestly ministry, celibate living, and devotion to prayer have not supplied. While the previous desolation was often filled with strong emotions of disappointment, regret, anger, frustration, and even fear, this second desolation (while it can admit to some of these same emotions) more often than not surfaces as an inchoate sense of ennui. "Where is this coming from?" the priest will often ask himself as this desolation takes hold. "What am I doing wrong? Why is this happening now after all these years?" he will further wonder. This new fathom of desolation opens up a deep emptiness inside of a priest that will make room for the intimacy and generativity that come from the indwelling of Christ. But how does one get to that deeper place of intimacy and generativity? The answer is never satisfying at first: by embracing the loneliness, the longings, and the limitations that are part of the inherent insufficiency of everyone's life.

In no way is the embrace of the incompleteness of one's life meant to be an exercise in masochistic spirituality. Rather, it is a purposeful surrendering once again to the unavoidable paschal process of priestly life and the essentially paschal nature of spiritual growth and development. I always say in spiritual direction to people experiencing some form of desolation who are quite annoyed with its repeated occurrence, "If you want to avoid desolation completely in life then become a totally shallow person." Only the unexamined life can skirt around the repeated dying and rising that need to happen, or at least hold them at bay longer. In the examined life, the heroic and faithful embrace of these paschal moments needs to be a *purposeful surrender*. It needs to be *purposeful* because the onset of another paschal death does not mean we will automatically discover and experience the deeper grace to which it is leading if we are not engaging it prayerfully with Christ. And it needs to be a *surrender* because, in the end, we cannot circumvent or end our paschal deaths; we need to let Christ take us through them with him. How does this happen?

First of all, this purposeful surrendering entails naming the Good Friday death that is going on—the sense of joy and fulfillment we experienced for years in priesthood is gone or has greatly diminished. This is when we need to draw from the heroic energy that is still within us; only now it has been sublated into a deeper level of our spiritual lives. As mentioned earlier in this chapter, Aquinas recognized how the Hero's initial courage to face and withstand whatever force needs to be opposed can later become the patience and forbearance to endure the difficulties in life that cannot be changed: in this case, the need to recognize and then give over to God's grace whatever has to die in us. This is especially so when emotionally and psychologically we do not want anything to die; instead we often want our previous experiences of consolation and satisfaction in priestly life and ministry to return.

Second, during this entrance into another level of desolation, the priest will need to recall the graced insights and previous consolations he received in the many years of his praying with Christ as a faithful companion. This is why keeping a journal of prayer can be a valuable resource. In moments of recollection with that journal, the priest can draw on the archetypal energy of the Faithful Servant with Christ that is also still within him. From this energy the priest in prayer can recognize the importance of now needing to be a Servant with Christ to his True Self who is now seeking to emerge more fully. In other words, the priest ought to recognize that he deserves to be ministered to by his own experiences with Christ in prayer and reflection. He needs to trust that Christ is by his side leading him into deeper waters where the man's True Self finds in Christ a more authentic level of his personhood, his priesthood, and his prayer.

This is important for two reasons. First of all, as noted earlier in the chapter, desolation can feel like excruciating loneliness. In describing St. Ignatius of Loyola's understanding of desolation, Mark Thibodeaux instructs: "The word *desolation* has its roots in the Middle English *de sole*, which translates as 'to be made alone, to be forsaken or abandoned.' Part of the experience of desolation is the sense that God is far distant from me. I can't feel a strong sense of God's presence."[12] I would add that in this second fathom of desolation a man can feel distant from himself and from others. Therefore, relying on the previous awareness of Christ's companionship in difficult moments of life, the priest in prayer can at least recognize in faith, if not in feeling, that Christ is his companion even in loneliness.

12. Mark E. Thibodeaux, *God's Voice Within: The Ignatian Way to Discover God's Will* (Chicago: Loyola Press, 2017), 19.

The second reason it is important for the priest to be a faithful, trusting servant with Christ even to himself is because this new desolation needs to be handled differently than previous ones. It may not present itself as a throbbing agitation that needs to be actively combatted as it might have when the Noble Hero was entering the paschal process. With the Faithful Servant now enduring his own Good Friday, what will surface is a sense of being stuck or mired in one place for a long time with no prospects of going anywhere. This is precisely when the priest needs to trust and believe that Christ is actively working within him, which means something very important and dynamic is occurring, though it does not feel that way.

Probing the Deeper Levels of Desolation and Insight

For those who take the spiritual life seriously, desolation is a very troubling, even frightening, experience. When it recurs and when it lingers, desolation can make priests who pray want to abandon prayer. It can lead priests to believe that priesthood has been an empty vocation, even an act of cruelty from a God who deceived them in their calling. It can even cause priests to question the value of their celibacy, the fruitfulness of their ministry, and the authenticity of everything they have tried to live. In introducing the notion of desolation in his *Spiritual Exercises*, St. Ignatius writes:

> By desolation I mean . . . obtuseness of soul, turmoil within it, and impulsive motion toward low and earthly things, or disquiet from various agitations and temptations. These move one toward lack of faith and leave one without hope and without love. One is completely listless, tepid, and unhappy, and feels separated from our Creator and Lord.[13]

But Ignatius offers several helpful guidelines for dealing with desolation and praying through it. These guidelines are quite insightful about how to prayerfully navigate through the pain of desolation. Mark Thibodeaux, in his wonderful text *God's Voice Within: The Ignatian*

---

13. St. Ignatius of Loyola, *The Spiritual Exercises of St. Ignatius of Loyola*, trans. George E. Ganss (St. Louis: The Institute of Jesuit Resources, 1992), 317.

Way to Discover God's Will, presents a fresh portrait of these guidelines. He makes them easily accessible to a contemporary audience and to pray-ers who might not be very well-versed in the dynamics of Ignatian spirituality. What he offers, however, is precisely what priests and all pray-ers need to access when their prayer life has dried up in the midst of desolation. Therefore, I list each of the guidelines that Thibodeaux offers, adding my own summary and suggestions:

1. *"Name the desolation."*
   When we name whatever darkness stirs inside of us we begin to lessen its grip on us and it eventually loses power over us. Remember how Jesus disarms the Gerasene Demoniac by asking the demon its name, which was "Legion." See Mark 5:1-13. Naming the desolation also keeps us from mistakenly identifying our discontent or malaise as a chronic condition that needs a permanent change in our state of life.

2. *"Avoid making changes or important decisions."*
   Our conflicted emotions or afflicted feelings will cry out for relief and try to get us to act in order to relieve them. This is when so many short-sided or ill-considered decisions are made by priests in crisis. This is where Ignatius's principle of *agere contra* comes in—act against the inclinations that arise for immediate and palpable relief to the desolation.

3. *"Rely on your support network."*
   Do not let the feelings of isolation isolate you. Stay connected to loved ones, friends, and priests who can be with you in what you are experiencing. This is where it is so crucial to have a spiritual director to whom you can be very frank and open and who will deal with you in the same way. Let all that the church has to offer by way of ritual, prayer, devotion, community, and wisdom bring comfort and relief to you.

4. *"Consider potential logistical, moral, or psychological problems."*
   Logistical: Is the time, manner, place, content of your prayer something that really works for you or does one or more of these elements need to change?

Moral: Are you engaged in a sinful pattern or habit that has begun to take its toll on your inner life? What needs to change in your actions or lifestyle that might be causing spiritual desolation? Is there something that you are holding or harboring inside of you that needs to be forgiven, reconciled, or healed?

Psychological: Is the desolation more a matter of depression, anxiety, grief, or some other psychological/emotional condition? Any of these above considerations would distinguish what you are going through as something other than true spiritual desolation and will need to be attended to in a different manner from what is being outlined here.

5. *"Be aware of the false 'angel of light.'"*

Do not give in to sudden bursts of inspiration or zeal that can lead you to good or religious acts that may seem acceptable and appropriate at first but are really coming from a conflicted place in your heart, mind, or spirit. To act this way will actually fuel the desolation, not lessen it. Here also Ignatius's principle of *agere contra* applies.

6. *"Be firm with the false spirit and work diligently."*

Stay resolute to be a man of prayer, allowing especially the obligation to pray the Liturgy of the Hours and the responsibility to celebrate the Eucharist to provide you a motive to pray, even if personal prayer is difficult at this time. Engage in more spiritual direction and more prayer than you have previously so as not to give the desolation more room in your inner life. Keep hard at work in ministry, even if your heart and spirit are not in it. Resist all temptations to do less, to withdraw, to withhold what you can offer others in ministry.

7. *"Be gentle, patient, and encouraging to yourself."*

Do not let the "shame voice" inside of you take over. This is the voice that comes from the wound inside each of us that tries to convince us we are worthless, unloved, even unlovable. Keep reminding yourself that what you are experiencing is a difficult part of an important process of becoming your True Self in Christ. This is how we might understand Ignatius's notion of "growing in full stature in Christ" mentioned earlier. Rest, relax,

play, enjoy but always within reason. Engage in the noble things
that have tended to refresh your spirit in a balanced way.

8. *"Have faith that God will make good use of this desolation."*[14]
It is important for Ignatius that we understand that God does
not cause desolation, but in God's providence he allows it in
order to bring us to a deeper experience of grace. Keep in mind
that God desires that we be joyful in life, but joy is a complex
amalgam of authenticity, happiness, and fulfillment. In desolation, in order for authenticity to become deeper or more advanced, the other aspects of joy might recede only to return later
but in a different way.

Faith and trust in God's desire that we be brought out of desolation
and into a deeper level of joy demand a lot of patience.

We have probably all heard the adage "It needs to happen in God's
way and in God's time." We have probably all preached on this concept
at one time or another. Yet this is precisely how consolation works—
God brings the faithful pray-er out of desolation and into a deeper
communion with him when the pray-er is made ready and open to
that deeper communion by the resolute and faith-filled struggle with
desolation. This does not happen only once; it happens repeatedly in
the spiritual life. Remember, as stated in chapter 1, the truly valiant
priest will die a thousand times before his death. The "second fathom
of desolation," however, is a pivotal moment within a whole series of
desolations (or deaths) that will happen for a priest (and anyone who
remains devoted to the interior workings of God). Likewise, this
critical desolation can lead to a pivotal consolation that occurs within
a whole series of consolations throughout priestly life and ministry.
The insights of St. Paul open the doorway to what this pivotal consolation is all about.

A reading of Acts of the Apostles along with the Pauline letters
reveal that St. Paul was a strong-willed, bright, zealous man who was
more than a little difficult at times. While his abilities and gifts were
clearly used by the Holy Spirit, Paul also had to struggle with his own

14. Thibodeaux, *God's Voice Within*, 63–101.

flaws, weaknesses, and limitations. Eventually, however, he recognized that God was at work in his struggles. St. Paul testifies:

> [T]o keep me from being too elated, a thorn was given me in the flesh, a messenger of Satan to torment me, to keep me from being too elated. Three times I appealed to the Lord about this, that it would leave me, but he said to me, "My grace is sufficient for you, for power is made perfect in weakness." So I will boast all the more gladly of my weaknesses, so that the power of Christ may dwell in me. Therefore, I am content with weaknesses, insults, hardships, persecutions, and calamities for the sake of the Christ; for whenever I am weak, then I am strong. (2 Cor 12:7-10)[15]

Clearly Paul knew desolation in his life and ministry, and it was not a one-time experience. Yet, Paul seems to have allowed his noble heroic drive for Christ and his faithful service with Christ to lead him to a newer energy in Christ. This did not happen without paschal deaths in his life. The portal to the resurrection of consolation and newness of life comes from embracing the cross. As St. Paul writes of himself: "I have been crucified with Christ; and it is no longer I who live, but it is Christ who lives in me. And the life I now live in the flesh, I live by faith in the Son of God who loved me and gave himself for me" (Gal 2:19-20).[16]

The pivotal consolation to which Paul is drawn arises out of a different archetypal energy than the Noble Hero or the Faithful Servant. Something has happened to Paul to lead him to the recognition that he no longer merely lives and works for Christ; he no longer simply preaches and ministers alongside Christ. Instead, he has discovered that all along Christ has been working in him, seeking to live in Paul more fully and for Paul to live in Christ more completely. This is the deepest stream in the currents of the spiritual life and clearly Paul has found it. But he did not find it apart from confronting the insufficiency of his own life and the limitations of his own abilities and talents. He was not led to the deeper waters by remaining in the more shallow

---

15. A portion of this reading appears in the *Liturgy of the Hours* for Friday Morning Prayer, Week 3.

16. This reading appears in the *Liturgy of the Hours* for Friday Morning Prayer, Week 4.

ones or by succumbing to the temptation to get out of the flowing current altogether. Instead, by faithfully engaging desolation, Paul was led by God through the portal of consolation. God desires the same for each of us whenever we experience despair in the midst of our steadfast dedication as Servants with Christ in priesthood. But it will happen in God's way and in God's time.

✠ CHAPTER THREE

A Humble Mystic *in* Christ *in* Me

Then the LORD *answered Job out of the whirlwind: . . .*
*   "Have you entered into the springs of the sea,*
*   or walked in the recesses of the deep?"*
—*Job 38:1, 16*

Jesus said, . . . "The water that I will give will become in
them a spring of water gushing up to eternal life."
—*John 4:13-14*

Finding Christ in the Deep

As God's query to Job makes clear, we cannot always know the ways of God, but it seems quite evident that God dwells in the deepest of the deep. Furthermore, in Jesus' words to the woman of Samaria, God reveals that this deepest of dwellings is actually within us, seeking to rise up from our core and bring us the true life God has always wanted for us. For many years in prayer, the Faithful Servant with Christ will have sought to enter the deeper places inside of him. At some point, however, he discovers that entering the deepest of the deep becomes not so much a matter of what further effort the priest needs to put into his prayer life as it is a matter of what Christ desires to do further in him. The call of the spiritual life at this point becomes less about *our "putting* out into the deep waters" and instead *Christ "pulling* us into the deepest of the deep."

Nonetheless, like the storyline of the Peter Benchley novel, "the deep" can seem like a very scary place to go. By this stage in his spiritual journey, when a priest has navigated the rough waters of a second fathom of desolation, he has come to recognize that inside of him lies a cavernous collection of the wounds of life, a profound emptiness and brokenness that has always been a part of who he is but into which he has never wanted to plunge. Furthermore, it now becomes painfully clear to him that this place in his deepest self will never be erased. Yet, he dares not go there by himself; it is Christ, the One who has been steadily at the side of the Servant priest all these years, who now beckons his prayerful companion to go with him into the wounds, into the chasm of emptiness, and into the deep current of the man's broken human condition because it is underneath all of those inner elements of one's personhood that the living waters of Christ's life spring up and bring the man to his own true life in Christ.

What do I mean by "brokenness" or "the wounds of life"? These terms can connote different things to different persons, but what they refer to is always a multifaceted reality at our deepest core, lying underneath our day-to-day conscious sense of our inner lives and our most operative self-images. Human brokenness encompasses all the ways that we are not who we were created to be by God, all the ways the False Self dominates over the True Self, and all the ways we do not live what God has made us capable of living. It is the fractured narrative of our lives. This would include our sinful inclinations and desires, especially compensatory needs for gratification, insatiable needs for affirmation or importance, unbridled needs for retribution or diminishment of others. Our human brokenness also includes, however, our limitations, our failings, our mistaken choices that have left their mark on our psyche as insecurities and unwarranted fears about life. Furthermore, our wounds come from all the ways we are affected by how others have failed to be who God created them to be and all the ways that others have failed to live what God has called them to live, that is, *their* fractured narratives. This would mean whatever things people have said or done (or failed to say or do) that made us feel that something was terribly wrong with us, most acutely in our pivotal developmental years growing up.

The most problematic effect that our wounds can have on us is the development of a "shame voice" inside of us. Unlike a healthy sense of shame that gives us a moral sense of limits and a needed jolt of reproof for what we have done wrong or for the good we have failed to do, the shame voice becomes a toxin inside of us that poisons our sense of self. In his book *Healing the Shame That Binds You*, John Bradshaw writes:

> Toxic shame, the shame that binds you, is experienced as the all-pervasive sense that I am flawed and defective as a human being. Toxic shame is no longer an emotion that signals our limits; it is a state of being, a core identity. Toxic shame gives you a sense of worthlessness, a sense of falling short as a human being. Toxic shame is a rupture of the self with the self.[1]

This often leads the shame-based person to adopt a False Self in order to escape from the defective sense of who he or she really is. This toxic shame is a searing psychological and emotional manifestation of the woundedness within all human beings.

In the church's theological tradition, the deep woundedness of the human condition has often been called "original sin." The church's tradition has also taught that through baptism one is freed from the effects of original sin. This is certainly true ontologically, since we are sacramentally and irrevocably united to Christ at our very core in the waters of baptism. Nevertheless, the effects of that original sin continue to exist experientially, psychologically, and emotionally throughout our lives. Because of our unity with Christ in the waters of rebirth, however, these effects never have the final word; they are not the ultimate power. Christ has the final word and it is one of healing love. Christ is the ultimate power to be discovered deep inside of us, when we enter into our brokenness and go into our wounds to find the One who is there with us underneath it all.

What makes this venture of entering into our brokenness or going into our wounds so daunting? First of all, no one instinctively desires to embrace the murkiest parts of oneself. Our instincts urge us to get away from whatever brings us harm or causes us pain. Furthermore, we spend so much emotional and psychological energy trying to *rise above* what is broken or wounded within us that to *go into* it all seems so counterintuitive and counterproductive. Priests are not immune from these resistances.

Second, no one enjoys admitting that pure motives have not always fueled their desires to do what they are doing in life. For priests, this will

---

1. John Bradshaw, *Healing the Shame That Binds You* (Deerfield, FL: Health Communications, 1988), 10. See also Wilkie Au and Noreen Cannon Au, *God's Unconditional Love: Healing Our Shame* (New York: Paulist Press, 2016), 15–24.

mean taking another look at their operative reasons for pursuing ordination, some of which began as ways of compensating for what were
perceived as missing pieces from their lives or limitations in themselves.
It takes years for one's hidden motives to be completely claimed by
Christ, whether they be one's known but unstated motives or a person's
unknown and unacknowledged needs for success, intimacy, making a
big difference in the world, or finding redemption, importance, prominence, security, identity, or even escape. A slow but steady "undoing"
of these shadowy motives is the nature of the paschal process.

Finally, the brokenness of the human condition of each priest surfaces from the murky depths at some point when he experiences the
loss of enthusiasm or motivation, the death of dreams, the emptiness
of prayer, the lack of effectiveness in ministry, the barrenness of lived
celibacy, the guilt of not being able to conquer a sinful pattern or habit,
the diminishment that comes with aging, or the anguish of suffering
one loss after another in one's personal life and priestly ministry. Again,
our instinct is to get beyond these feelings and experiences as soon as
possible but certainly not to plunge into them. Even worse, for some
priests, when these elements of the broken human condition surface,
they default to their entrenched predisposition to avoid the interior
life. They are prone to agree with the sentiment that "too much introspection is a dangerous thing," which, I have often found, is really
coded language for "*any* introspection is a dangerous thing." When
priests find themselves wanting to avoid the depths of their heart,
psyche, and inner spirit, what they need is a different perspective on
what actually is going on inside of them. It would be good for them to
come to the recognition that in their deepest deep is Christ-in-their-
brokenness, whose oneness with them seeks to well up within them
as the life-giving water of their true selves and their true life in Christ.

Another different and hopeful perspective comes from Thomas
Merton; he sees the willingness to admit honestly and then surrender
willingly our fractured narratives over to grace as an amazing process,
which he likens to Advent. For Merton, Advent is not merely a liturgical season; it is the nature of lifelong conversion in one's whole spiritual biography. In a wonderful article on the meaning of Advent as
both a beginning and an ending, a future hope and a current transformation, Merton writes: "The Advent mystery in our own lives is the
beginning of the end of all, in us, that is not yet Christ. It is the begin-

ning of the end of unreality. And that is surely a cause of joy! But unfortunately we are clinging to our unreality, we prefer the part to the whole, we continue to be fragments, we do not want to be one."[2]

The call to oneness with Christ that is inherent in the spiritual biography of priests constantly beckons us not to be frightened of the broken self that emerges but instead to surrender whatever has not yet been fully conformed to the priestly heart of Christ, to the power of transforming communion with him. This communion, however, comes not merely from engaging in ministry and being faithful to prayer as our earlier archetypal energies allowed. Instead, the most intimate level of communion comes from a very humbling journey to the deep dwelling place of Christ inside of us, Emmanuel-in-our-inner-core. If we are to lead others in their own Advent process of transformation into Christ, then we must undergo it as well, and with more diligence. Our constant Advent journey to the place inside of our lives where Christ seeks to come alive in us never allows us to stay too long in one place. It calls for us to journey further in the spiritual life, into mysticism; for only the mystic can hear the beckoning of Christ from the deepest deep, and only the mystic can see through the dark and murky depths of our wounded human nature and discover that those depths are precisely where Christ seeks to come to us.

The Priestly Desire of Christ

We are not destined to be plagued by a constant sense of fragmentation (as Merton warns above) or separation from the God who loves us or from who we are meant to be. Before he died, Jesus made it clear that he desires that his disciples discover that his truest way of being with them will come from his dwelling within them and their dwelling within him. It is because of this mutual indwelling that our calling to become a priest will not allow us to stay forever at that place inside of us where we can be a Noble Hero for Christ and a Faithful Servant with Christ. Instead, Christ, who dwells in our core, will constantly beckon us to a deeper level of priesthood that calls us to become a Humble Mystic in Christ, an archetypal energy that is already within

2. Thomas Merton, "The Advent Mystery," *Worship* 38 (December 1963): 17–25, at 22.

our first moment of yes to Christ's call. Unlike our earlier moments of yes to Christ, however, at this point in our spiritual biography our yes to our priestly vocation does not come with any form of celebration or external acclaim; it is not heralded by others or often talked about when priests gather together; it is not even insisted on by the institutional church. Yet, it is the deepest layer of our original yes to priesthood, and it can make all the difference.

At our ordination, we gave our consent to the bishop to conform our lives to the sacred mysteries we would celebrate, and the bishop prayed that God, who had begun the good work in us, would bring it to fulfillment. Then, after consecrating our hands with chrism, the bishop presented us with a paten of bread and a chalice of wine instructing us:

> Receive the oblation of the holy people, to be offered to God.
> Understand what you do, imitate what you celebrate,
> and conform your life to the mystery of the Lord's cross.[3]

In that exchange with the bishop we assented to live inside the depths of the paschal mystery of Christ, and, whether we realized it or not, this meant entering the depths of our own brokenness with Christ. We consented to letting God do far more with our inner lives than we were yet aware of in order to bring to fulfillment his Son's desire to be intimately connected with the depths of our priestly heart, mind, and spirit.

With all this talk about entering the depths of our brokenness and embracing the paschal mystery, some may object and ask: Does it have to be this way? Wouldn't it be better for us to just stay focused on the joys and blessings of priestly life and ministry? What about adopting a more vigorous capacity for gratitude and stop looking at what is hurting or disheartened within us or disappointing and frustrating about priesthood? Some conclude, then, that these modes of prayer would do much to lighten our hearts and free us from the grip of our wounds and limitations as human beings.

There is some value to these suggestions; they capture some important elements in the crucial foundation that has to be laid in our

---

3. *Rites of Ordination of a Bishop, of Priests, and of Deacons*, Second Typical Edition (Washington, DC: USCCB, 2003), no. 135.

spiritual lives in order to deepen our encounter with Christ. For instance, before we can prayerfully enter into our "wounds," we need first to become anchored in the realization that God is always holding on to us in love and that we can face whatever turmoil or distress comes our way because God is holding on to us. This allows us to recognize that nothing we discover in the murky recesses of our inner lives can ever be more forceful than the power of God's constant love for us. Practicing daily gratitude for the blessings from God in our lives is an important way to remain anchored in that realization. In addition, deliberately recalling all the ways that God has sustained us in priesthood over the years and all the ways in the past that God has been for us what we needed in ministry are important components in our spiritual lives: they will do much to keep us firm in our belief that nothing we face in the world or in ourselves do we ever face alone. Nonetheless, a constancy of gratitude and a steadfast recognition of the grace of God in our lives will not erase our woundedness or eliminate our broken self; nor do they completely silence the shame voice. This is precisely why Christ beckons us to go into our brokenness with him and discover his abiding presence deep within. Even more, it is the earnest desire of Christ that we meet him there; he expressed this in his "priestly prayer" the night before he died.

As he gathered with his disciples in the Upper Room to share a final meal before his death, Jesus prayed on their behalf to the Father:

> As you, Father, are in me and I am in you, may they also be in us. . . . The glory that you have given me I have given them, so that they may be one, as we are one, I in them and you in me, that they may become completely one, so that the world may know that you have sent me and have loved them even as you have loved me. Father, I desire that those also, whom you have given me, may be with me where I am. (John 17:21-24)

This prayer reveals the priestly desire of Christ that those who minister in his name may experience his indwelling presence and that his presence within them may awaken their sense of being loved by the Father. Furthermore, the priestly desire of Christ is that his disciples be drawn into communion with God and with each other. In other words, the more they discover Christ deep within themselves, they will recognize in Christ their oneness with God and with each other. This is not merely an emotionally felt, cognitively recognized, or ministerially enacted oneness; it is a oneness on the deepest level of their being— their most inner core. Entering that inner core—that wounded, deepest self—is where they fulfill the desire of Christ that they "may be with me where I am." Furthermore, it is from that wounded, deepest self that their oneness with all others in their own brokenness happens (more on this in the next chapter).

The context for this priestly prayer of Jesus is important. His passion is about to unfold; indeed, Judas Iscariot has already left the table to do what he was going to do (see John 13:21-30). With Jesus' impending passion and death, the manner in which his disciples have been experiencing his tangible presence is about to unravel. Therefore, Jesus needs to prepare them for a new way of encountering him and a new manner of being sustained by a vivid and tangible connection to him. Jesus' priestly prayer includes the words to the Father: "And now I am no longer in the world, but they are in the world, and I am coming to you" (John 17:11). Jesus continues, "But now I am coming to you, and I speak these things in the world so that they may have my joy made complete in them" (John 17:13). *There's the key!* Jesus does not want his disciples to know only fleeting happiness or ephemeral bliss. He desires that they experience *his* joy that comes from his deep communion with the Father. It is a joy that he offers to them as his passion begins; therefore, it is a joy that comes from Jesus' own embrace of all that is wounded, hurting, and painful in the world and in each human life. The offer of Christ's joy comes from entering Christ's embrace of the broken human condition. And that is the place where Jesus is to be found.[4]

---

4. The Synoptic Gospels offer details in their Last Supper accounts of Jesus establishing the Eucharist as his new mode of tangible presence for the disciples after his death and resurrection. John's gospel makes the case for this eucharistic presence of Christ in Jesus' Bread of Life Discourse in chapter 6. With the notion of the eucharistic presence of Christ already well established earlier in his gospel, John seems to want to lead his readers through the Last Supper Discourse to the experience of the fruit of the eucharistic presence of Christ, which includes the inner tangibility of Christ's presence (his indwelling presence) that the Eucharist nourishes and strengthens. For more on this see Xavier Léon-Dufour, "The Eucharist According to John," chapter 13 in his *Sharing the Eucharistic Bread: The Witness of the New Testament* (New York: Paulist Press, 1982), 248–77.

Not only does John's passion narrative reveal this connection between oneness with Christ's passion and oneness with Christ's joy; so too does his resurrection narrative. In John's account of the postresurrection appearances of Christ we find the encounter between the risen Lord and the doubting apostle Thomas (see John 20:24-28). What convinces Thomas that Jesus has indeed risen from the dead and that Jesus is truly his mighty Lord and God is the invitation by the risen Christ to touch his wounds. The reality of the resurrection is found by embracing the wounds that remain in Christ. This encounter reveals that woundedness is not a distraction, deviation, or detour from our communion with Christ; it is the very point of entry. To touch *his* wounds is to discover communion with him in *our* wounds. He is in our wounds as surely as we are in his, and it is from our wounds that Christ desires to bring to life the effects of the resurrection—the welling up of our true life from deep within us that allows us to come to full stature in Christ. This means that, ironically, it is by prayerfully entering what is deeply broken within us that Christ's joy is made complete in us—a joy that sustains us even when emotional happiness, meaningful relationships, and ministerial fulfillment fade or falter. Furthermore, by entering our inner wounds to find Christ within us, we begin to live more fully *in* Christ, not just *for* him and not just *with* him.

Sublating the Servant into the Mystic

As was doubting Thomas's rebuke by Jesus, our own drawing near to his wounds and our own brokenness can be a very humbling experience, even frightening at times, because it means something about us has to die. Some lingering aspect of our False Self has to come apart so that more of our True Self can come to life. It could be a false persona that we still maintain or an incomplete self-conception in which we hide from own woundedness. Richard Rohr puts it this way:

> The False Self has no substance, no permanence, no vitality, only various forms of immediate gratification. . . . Again, it is not usually bad or evil, but just inadequate to the big questions of love, death, suffering, God, and any notion of infinity. God allows and uses all our diversionary tactics to get us to the full destination. This is how perfect and patient love is. God probably knows

we are procrastinators rather than perpetrators. The True Self
will surely have doubts about the unknown. . . . But as such, the
True Self is not afraid of death. . . . The Risen Christ in you always knows that it will never lose anything real by dying. . . .
Once you know you are sharing in *the force field of resurrection,*
you can always draw on it, live within it, and move out from it.[5]

The Noble Hero has trouble entering his own wounds; he seeks to
carry on in spite of them in order to transform a wounded world for
Christ. The Faithful Servant, while aware of his wounds, seeks more
to be with Christ in caring for the wounds of others. It takes the archetypal energy of the Humble Mystic to recognize that his own
wounds are the pathway to life-giving communion with Christ. The
Mystic peers into the deep and murky recesses of his own broken
personhood and sees the risen Christ dwelling there and beckoning
him, "Touch my wounds, for you are in my wounds and I am in yours."
This encounter is where Christ the Priest meets each priest in the
core of his being. It is where Christ the Priest claims everything that
each priest really is as a broken human being, not merely how he
functions within the church, not merely how he is regarded and seen
by others, not merely in what he does for the church and for the world,
but who he really is and always has been, long before he first heard
the call of Christ.

Once a priest can recognize in faith that the power of resurrection
is to be discovered in his own fractured narrative, he can then begin
to enter more confidently into a new chapter of his spiritual biography.
This will mean, however, that he will need to embrace a new manner
of prayer. The communion between the risen-but-wounded Christ
and the wounded-and-prayerful priest happens less from a form of
active prayer and more from a confident surrender into silence. The
priest's previous forms of active prayer as a Noble Hero and Faithful
Servant should serve to reassure him that the church and world still
need him to pray and that Christ is with him in his prayer. Now, however, the priest is to commune with Christ in a much deeper way—a
way that has been adopted by mystics.

5. Richard Rohr, *Immortal Diamond: The Search for Our True Self* (San Francisco: Jossey-Bass, 2013), 143–44; emphasis in original.

Karl Rahner is often quoted as stating, "The Christian of the future will be a mystic or will not exist at all."[6] Most people, priests included, are intimidated by the word "mystic" because they often see it as a description for a type of spiritual person who is so completely different from the way they see themselves as spiritual persons. Yet, in a real sense, every Christian man and woman is called to be a mystic, for mysticism is living one's life out of the interior dwelling place of Christ, who in turn draws us into himself. It is accurate to recognize that we cannot achieve mysticism, but we can allow Christ's Spirit to draw us into the important, life-giving, and deeply consoling inner mystical communion with Christ. Being drawn into silence is the key to this mysticism.

Hopefully, years of praying with Christ as a tangible Companion in every dimension of priestly service will give the priest assurance that becoming silent in prayer will not feel like abandonment, loneliness, or emptiness. Instead, what is happening is that Emmanuel is claiming more and more of the man's personhood so that God-with-us can be more fully revealed in the man's most authentic priesthood, thus bringing to life the True Self within the true priest underneath all the doing of pastoral ministry, all the reciting of prayers, all the proclaiming and preaching the Word, all the planning and preparing for sacred rites and liturgies, all the sitting with and counseling or consoling others. Underneath all the energy of activity is the mystery of Emmanuel—God-with-us-in-our-deepest-core.

Though this may be the case, the lingering energy of both the Hero archetype, who wants to accomplish great things for Christ, and the Servant archetype, who wants to do good for others with Christ, makes it hard to trust that Christ now asks of them a radical "non-accomplishment" and an unfamiliar "non-doing" in their priesthood. This reversal of energy into stillness and silence is indeed a challenge; yet it is where the deeper currents in the spiritual life will always lead us. We all know dedicated priests who, after retirement, will excitedly declare, "I finally get to pray more," or, "I am finally developing the spiritual life I always wanted." Though they may not state it in this manner, these men are experiencing the gift of mysticism. This gift is,

6. Karl Rahner, "Concern for the Church," in *Theological Investigations*, vol. 20, trans. Edward Quinn (New York: Crossroad, 1981), 149.

however, neither something reserved only for later in life nor even something saved only for after a priest retires. Christ from deep within us is beckoning us at every stage of life and priestly service to quiet ourselves and embrace the power of stillness.

During Wednesday Evening Prayer of Week 2 in the Liturgy of the Hours, the priest prays at the beginning of Psalm 62, "In God alone is my soul at rest; my help comes from him." A better translation of that verse, along with a later passage in Psalm 62, reads, "For God alone my soul waits in silence; from him comes my salvation. . . . For God alone my soul waits in silence, for my hope is from him" (vv. 1, 5). In another psalm from Tuesday Evening Prayer, Week 3, the priest prays:

> O Lord, my heart is not proud
> Nor haughty my eyes.
> I have not gone after things too great
> Nor marvels beyond me.
>
> Truly I have set my soul
> in silence and peace.
> As a child rests in his mother's arms,
> even so my soul. (Ps 131:2)

These are the words of a pray-er whose heroic and servant energies have undergone a true paschal process leading to the need for stillness and silence.

In his book *Into the Silent Land*, Martin Laird wonderfully reassures us:

> Because God is the ground of our being, the relationship between creature and Creator is such that, by sheer grace, separation is not possible. The fact that most of us experience throughout most of our lives a sense of absence or distance from God is the great illusion that we are caught up in; it is the human condition. The sense of separation from God is real, but the meeting of stillness reveals that this perceived separation does not have the last word. . . . For when the mind is brought to stillness, and all our strategies of acquisition have dropped, a deeper truth presents

itself: we are and always have been one with God and we are all one in God (Jn 17:21).[7]

Further reassuring us is a forthright assertion by Laird about our human predisposition toward stillness; he states: "Communion with God in the silence of the heart is a God-given capacity. . . . [W]e are built to commune with God."[8]

For priests who develop more strongly the capacity for discursive prayer (e.g., reciting the Divine Office, presiding at the Eucharist, leading devotional prayers, engaging in *lectio divina* and other forms of meditation on the Scriptures, including Ignatian prayer), the entrance into nondiscursive stillness can seem a bit daunting and anything but a "God-given capacity." Furthermore, for priests who have spent so much of their lives in active mode, the ability to pull their mind, heart, and imagination away from the energy of *doing* for Christ and *doing* with Christ to the silent depth of simply *being* with Christ can feel at first like meaningless idleness. But into the stillness we must go, for it is there that the archetypal energy of the Faithful Servant with Christ becomes sublated into the deeper archetypal energy of the Humble Mystic in Christ who is in him.

Entering into Silence

When Jesus called his disciples to "put out into the deep water" (Luke 5:4), he was offering paradigmatic instructions not only for the nature of the ministry they were about to embark on but also for the necessary course of their spiritual lives sustaining them in that ministry. In deeper waters, the malaise or dissatisfaction that surfaces within the ministry and prayer of the Faithful Servant priest is led to a more profound grace that is the beginning of the end of all in the priest that is not yet Christ. But the current in that deeper fathom of the spiritual life flows differently from those of the other levels of prayer in the priest's life up to this point. This deeper current flows into a silent place of the indwelling Christ where there are no words,

---

7. Martin Laird, *Into the Silent Land: A Guide to the Christian Practice of Contemplation* (Oxford: Oxford University Press, 2006), 15–16.

8. Ibid., 1.

no keen insights, no rush of emotional consolation. There is only the ineffable and often subtle depth of intimacy with the One who knows us in our utter brokenness, loves us, and remains in us.

As pointed out earlier, it is important for the priest to recognize that his entering into this level of stillness is a continuation of the yes he said to Christ and to the church so many years before. It entails continuity with the desire to be the Noble Hero, for it takes heroic belief to trust in the power of "not doing" and it takes noble courage to stay with prayer that can be uncomfortable since its "rewards" are not always immediately tangible. Likewise, the call to enter into stillness is an extension of the priest's willingness to be the Faithful Servant with Christ. Only now the Divine Companion is found in the core of the Servant in his stillness and not merely shoulder-to-shoulder with him in his ministry.

In addition, the call of Christ to his disciples to "put out into deep water" is not a different call from when Christ responded to his first disciples' query, "Where are you staying?" (John 1:38). Jesus' response, "Come and see" (John 1:39), is the same invitation, for the deeper waters of the spiritual life are precisely where Christ dwells in the lives of his disciples. Jesus is at home in our deepest core. This is another wonderful example of the scriptural device of inclusion that we saw in chapter 2 with Matthew's gospel, only now we see it in John's gospel. This fourth account of the public life of Jesus begins, as noted above, with his invitation to would-be disciples to come to his home. By inclusion, in John's gospel the public life of Jesus draws to a close when he reveals to his disciples that his home is within them (John 17:23).

Applying this inclusion to priestly spirituality we recognize that the eventual disquietude that even the most Faithful Servant experiences after years of prayer and ministry is really a furthering of the call by Christ to be at home with him in priesthood. For the Mystic, Christ the High Priest dwells deep inside of him, deep within his humble, broken, faithful, heroic, and prayerful life as a priest of the church. Therefore, the Mystic now sees priesthood as arising not only from ordination by the church but from within the humble dwelling place of Christ deep inside a man's True Self. The Mystic recognizes that priesthood is exercised not only in the doing of ministry but in the radical "non-doing" that occurs in stillness and silence in which a priest enters into communion with the indwelling of Christ-the-Priest-with-him-and-in-him. This is priesthood that is not seen or rewarded or active, though it is very operative within the seen, admired, and active ministry of a good priest. It is the priesthood of a man's life that is now, in the words of St. Paul, "hidden with Christ in God" (Col 3:3). The priest's deepest deep is the home of Emmanuel.

We celebrate the coming of Emmanuel by singing about a "silent night" when "all is calm, all is bright." Instinctively, we realize that the encounter with Emmanuel calls us to silence in order to illuminate the once hidden reality of intimacy with God. While making reference to the birth of Emmanuel, the philosopher Max Picard writes:

> This event is so utterly extraordinary and so much against the experience of reason and against everything the eye has seen, that [we are] not able to make response to it in words. A larger silence lies between this event and [us], and in this silence [the human] approaches the silence that surrounds God Himself. [Humanity] and mystery first meet in silence. . . . The silence of God is transformed by love into the Word. The Word of God is a self-giving silence, giving itself to [humanity].[9]

From the beginning, Christ intended for us to meet him in silence, whereby stillness of mind and heart, body and spirit become encounter with Emmanuel.

The experience of Elijah the prophet as he is fleeing the wrath of King Ahab is a wonderfully paradigmatic moment for our journey through silence into our core where we find Christ (see 1 Kgs 19:9-13).[10] God instructs Elijah to go to Mount Horeb, the most holy place of encounter with God. As Elijah stands there, he sees and hears a strong, driving wind that breaks mountains and rocks before him, but God is not in this cataclysmic display. Then Elijah experiences an earthquake, but God is not in the upheaval. Finally, Elijah hears "a tiny whispering sound," according to the New American Bible, which we use for our Lectionary. The translation of the New Revised Standard Version, however, states that God comes to Elijah as "a sound of sheer

9. Max Picard, *The World of Silence* (Wichita, KS: Eighth Day Press, 2002), 227, 230.
10. This passage is proclaimed in the liturgy on the Nineteenth Sunday in Ordinary Time, Year A.

silence" (1 Kgs 19:12). Applying this scriptural passage to our own journey in the spiritual life, as our priestly spirituality grows and deepens, after we have endured one difficulty after another and withstood one perilous assault on our sense of security and consolation after another, in the manner of Elijah, we discover that Christ is met most forcefully and effectively not in what smashes our hopes and dreams, not in what drives away our sense of complacency and security, and not in what shakes our world and causes our hearts to tremble. Instead, Christ is intimately known in sheer silence.

This is the Jesus Christ who retreats into silence after hearing the news of the death of John the Baptist (Matt 14:13). It is the Christ who needs to be alone after bringing healing and food to a large crowd of people in need (Matt 14:22-12). It is the Christ whose own pleas to God on the night before he dies are met with silence (Mark 14:35-40) and who stands defiantly in silence before Pilate (John 19:9). Christ repeatedly moves into silence as he engages human brokenness in public ministry. Likewise, as Christ most fully embraces that brokenness in his passion, he enters into a profound silence in the tomb. Ironically, Christ, who is the Word-made-flesh, is also the Word-made-silence. All that Christ seeks to communicate to us as love, hope, mercy, strength, and joy is discovered when words cease, when activity halts, and when stillness is prayerfully engaged. Silence is the privileged place of communion with Christ. Yet that communion is not easily discovered.

As one tries to prayerfully engage silence with a prayer word or phrase, all of one's afflicted emotions (all the recognized and felt aspects of one's own personal brokenness and woundedness) and all the responsibilities of one's life tend to rise up as distractions. By drawing those distractions in to the prayer word, one can actually be led to the silence beneath them where pure Loving Divine Presence is discovered. This is the Presence of the Word-made-flesh-made-silence. In this way, we can recognize that at our core we are broken human beings and always will be—that is, brokenness is a constitutive part of our personhood, including our deepest self. From this recognition we can then find communion with Christ in the silence underneath our brokenness, not in spite of it, not when its effects might recede, not after we might be free of it, and not only in brokenness that is "out there" in others or in the world or in what we are living in the external life and doing in ministry.

Many spiritual writers offer great advice about how to enter silence in contemplation or centering prayer. They insist on the need to persist in efforts at moving past our distractions (or better, engaging our distractions) in order to enter the quieting of the mind and heart that is silent prayer. Martin Laird wrote his treatise *Into the Silent Land* as a very helpful guide for all who recognize the need to embrace silent prayer. Throughout his text, Laird leads the reader through the process of engaging in contemplative, nondiscursive prayer. His instructions begin with breathing slowly and deeply, all the while focusing the busy mind on a prayer word or phrase. As distractions come, and they will, the prayer word or phrase pulls the distractions into the self-emptying prayer and into the silence underneath all thoughts, all afflicted emotions, all unsettling worries that are vying for attention.[11]

Of particular significance for priests, whose lives are often so busy, is the need to quiet the mind of constantly planning or replaying the obligations of ministry. Furthermore, in facing the incompleteness and insufficiency of his own life, the priest will need to get past the regrets, the longings, the hurts, and the gnawing doubts that have been rising up within him as the Faithful Servant undergoes the paschal process. Laird calls these kinds of distractions to our prayer our "inner noise and mental clutter."[12] He reminds us that they lead us to a lie that our broken human condition entails a separation from God, others, and even ourselves. The content of the lie, in Laird's words, becomes "an inner video that plays again and again and steals our attention so that we overlook the simplest truths: we are already one with God. The Christian contemplative tradition addresses this very problem by exposing the lie and introducing stillness to the mental chatter."[13] In the stillness what has felt like loneliness, disintegration, emptiness becomes communion with the indwelling Christ.

Living Priesthood from the Indwelling Presence of Christ

Once a priest as the Mystic-in-Christ has begun to befriend silent prayer, his "afflicted emotions" do not miraculously come to an end, but he learns to hold them inside of himself in a different manner. Once a Mystic regularly enters into contemplative stillness, he will not

---

11. Laird, *Into the Silent Land*, 34–42.

12. Ibid., 29. See also Laird's *A Sunlit Absence: Silence, Awareness, and Contemplation* (Oxford: Oxford University Press, 2011).

13. Laird, *Into the Silent Land*, 29.

see all his problems fade, all the difficult issues or persons in his life go away, or all the internal disquiet or longing that he experiences cease. Instead, he will engage them in a different way. Furthermore, once a Mystic seeks to enter the deepest deep where Christ dwells within him, he will not be immune from further moments of desolation, worry, confusion, doubt, or loneliness down the road. He will, however, know how to navigate his way through them with a different sense of what is unfolding.

With those caveats in mind, it is also important to assert that deep mystical communion with Christ can wonderfully change the way a priest experiences priesthood on the inside, and it can positively affect how he lives priesthood on the outside, though the differences might only be known to him. For instance, the more a priest develops a habit of silent prayer, the more he is able to draw all the unresolved and unsolvable problems in priestly ministry into a place of simply being with them with Christ in whom his priesthood dwells and who dwells in his priesthood. This experience of communion can allow the priest to recognize that he cannot resolve any problem on his own; he must meet them with Christ. In addition, he may be able to come to the peaceful discernment that some of the problems in ministry cannot be resolved at all and that he simply needs to bring them into Christ's loving Presence and let Christ hold them for him.

Likewise, the more a priest engages in the mysticism of stillness, the less he tries to "fix" everything that continues to be "wrong" with himself on the inside or what he does not like about himself on the outside. Instead, he discovers how much he is unconditionally loved in all of his brokenness and woundedness, as the True Self both he and Christ know him to be. Furthermore, the priest is able to draw all the toxic messages from the shame voice into his silence and allow the power of the underlying, ineffable Presence of Love to quiet what is being said so falsely. Moreover, the priest can finally let go of seeing priesthood in any way as a compensation for his own shortcomings or as a substitution for what has been missing or lacking in his life. Instead, all of his shortcomings and limitations, all that he continues to long for and grieves not having—all of this is drawn into the man's oneness in priesthood with Christ, who claims every aspect of the man and lives as Love within everything that makes the priest who he truly is *and who he is not*. From this union can rise up a wonderful sense of freedom and genuine self-acceptance that comes from the truth about himself that Love speaks to him. When this kind of self-awareness is more firmly within a priest's heart and mind, then he finds that he is less prone to overreact to personalities or situations that expose his insecurities and self-doubts. He is less susceptible to compensatory or addictive behaviors and attractions. Finally, he is less likely to be undone by moments of failure or ineffectiveness in ministry.

A further possible outcome from regular engagement with silence is the establishment of a healthier pace in priestly life and ministry. All the effort it takes to engage in silence day after day, with its inherent struggles with distractions, exposes a man's capacity for being still that he would never have recognized or admitted before. Once it is exposed, it will crave attention. In addition, in the stillness what is really important and what is not so important become clearer because of the intensity with which they present themselves as distractions to prayer. By engaging them head on and drawing them through the prayer word or phrase into the silence with Christ, a priest can emerge from the silent prayer with a better discernment about what does need his proximate attention and what he can put aside for the time being or what he can delegate to someone else altogether.

Another contribution from silence toward a healthier pace in priestly life and ministry comes from the antidote it provides for a man whose life has been so much on display and whose role is often the center of attention at worship, meetings, and parish functions. Silence has the wonderful potential of awakening a genuine desire within a prayerful priest that is often eclipsed by the public nature of his ministry. In silence, a priest can finally give in to his longing to become "less" in life, to recede into the background at times and embrace the "little way" of St. Thérèse of Lisieux. Silence allows the priest to become so one with Christ that he discovers in that internal oneness what St. John the Baptist discovered in his own relationship to the Christ he heralded, that he might decrease so that Christ may increase (see John 3:30). The peace and sustenance found in silence allows the priest to consider appropriate ways to decrease without shirking his responsibilities or becoming an absentee or disinterested shepherd. This draw toward decrease can also inform how a priest handles the inevitable diminishment and limitations that come from aging, the new reality of retirement, or the unexpected effects of a chronic illness or a major injury.

Finally, the greatest gift that silence brings to the life of a priest is the silence itself. In the deepest waters of stillness one experiences a flow of intimacy with the Loving Presence of Christ that cannot always be expressed. This ineffable encounter is its own reward, and for each priest it takes on the texture and tone of the distinctiveness of his own particular brokenness, woundedness, and openness and longing to be Christ within him. What one finds in that most secret inner place often cannot be described to others, nor does it need to be. In the silence, the Mystic simply delights in being with Christ, who lives within him in a manner unique to the Mystic and who draws the Mystic to live more fully in Christ. This is how and where silence becomes the source of the ultimate generativity of a priest's life—the giving of himself as his True Self who lives in Christ who lives in him.

Discovering Eucharistic Generativity as a Priest

The generativity that a Mystic in Christ discovers in and through silence can inform his commitment to celibacy in a deeper way, and the Eucharist becomes a much more profound experience of communion than ever before with Christ and with the broken people a priest serves day after day. This is not to say that a priest, before entering the stage of the Mystic in Christ, had never found any fulfillment in celibacy nor any deep meaning within the Eucharist in his years of ordained ministry. The Eucharist is the primary source of sustenance and identity in every chapter of a priest's life. In addition, throughout a priest's spiritual journey, lived celibacy provides a richly meaningful context for the exercise of priestly ministry and a uniquely powerful sense of kinship with the manner in which the celibate Christ gave of himself in his own public ministry. Nevertheless, since the Eucharist and celibacy are complex realities, there is always something more, something deeper to be discovered about them so that they can more fully inform one's priesthood. When a priest engages the Mystic archetypal energy of his inner life, he soon discovers so much more to the Eucharist and to celibacy.

Within the celebration of the Eucharist the words of institution begin to identify a powerful oneness all priests have with Christ. Jesus' offer of his broken body "given for you" (Luke 22:19) and his blood "poured out for many" (Mark 14:24) reminds us that it is Christ's brokenness and self-giving that we ingest in the Eucharist. In offering, consuming, and distributing the Eucharist day after day, priests are much more able to embrace the sacredness of all that they have ever truly been but also failed to be as good but imperfect human beings, dedicated but flawed priests, experienced but not always successful pastors. In turn, they are much more capable of drawing the People of God into this same eucharistic mystery within their spiritual lives. How does this happen?

First of all, priests need to realize that it is their own brokenness that is baked into that bread and sublated into the Body of Christ. It is their own imperfect manner of emptying themselves for others that ferments within that wine and is sublated into the Blood of Christ. Thus, the Eucharist truly becomes their communion with Christ in brokenness and in being poured out. In the very first extant Christian writing on the Eucharist, St. Paul reminds us, "The cup of blessing that we bless, is it not a sharing in the blood of Christ? The bread that we break, is it not a sharing in the body of Christ?" (1 Cor 10:16). It is imperative that those who preside at the Eucharist allow their own eucharistic spirituality to come to this sense of communion with Christ in brokenness, for it is their role to help the people of God to do the same. Only a priest who finds his own brokenness sublated into the eucharistic mystery can lead others into the recognition of the same eucharistic sublation of their own brokenness.

To this end, the practice of silence becomes crucial because it allows a priest no longer to wince at his own brokenness or to try to bury within distractions, desires, and compensatory behaviors what has been wounded or left wanting in his own sense of himself. Instead, as described above, in the practice of silence the wounded priest meets the wounded Christ, the brokenness of an ordinary man is assumed into the brokenness of the indwelling Savior. Therefore, silent prayer reveals more clearly that when a priest takes up broken-bread-become-Christ into his hands, he is also taking up his broken self in communion with Christ. And when he eats that broken-bread-become-Christ, the sacred food that enters his body nourishes and strengthens the deep, inner communion he has with Christ in the core of his being—the sacred place of encounter with Christ that has opened up to him.

Second, when informed by the Eucharist that he constantly cele-brates, a priest's practice of silence uncovers how underneath all the "doing" of ministry in a priest's life—underneath all the worries, re-grets, responsibilities, heartaches, projects, affirmation, consolation, and joys—underneath everything into which he has emptied himself out lies the Presence of Love who is always poured out for us but never emptied. The significance of this silent encounter with that poured-out Love is found in the Eucharist when the priest takes up the chalice of poured-out wine that is now the poured-out Blood of Christ. As he drinks in all that Christ pours out in his love, that love seeps down into the ineffable place of encounter with Christ in a priest's core and it nurtures and enlivens the priest's own capacity for pouring out love without ever being emptied of it within himself. Thus, the deeper the priest's sense of intimacy with Christ in the Eucharist, the more gen-erative his celibate life becomes. What he generates from his "Eucha-ristized" celibacy is the capacity to bring God's People into their own ineffable place of encounter with the love of Christ—a love that is constantly poured out into them and a love that desires to be poured out into the world through them.

I find within the Psalter of the Liturgy of the Hours an interesting line that creates for me an intersection between the Eucharist and celibacy. In Psalm 116, which is prayed at Sunday Evening Prayer 1, Week 3, the psalmist describes that after his experience of utter de-spair, God came to his rescue. He then prays,

> How can I repay the Lord
> for his goodness to me?
> The cup of salvation I will raise;
> I will call on the Lord's name.
> My vows to the Lord I will fulfill
> before all his people.

This cup of blessing that is taken up in gratitude to God becomes the pledge of living what one vowed and promised. For the priest, every time he takes up the eucharistic cup of salvation and slakes in all that the Love of Christ pours out into him, he finds the capacity to live even more vibrantly his vow to pour out love as a celibate man. For that is what celibacy must always be—a particular manner in which one's communion with the love of Christ is offered for the sake and well-being of others. It is never mere singleness (or bachelorhood), and it is certainly not *repressed* sexuality, for sexuality is the God-given capacity within all human beings precisely meant to *express* themselves and give themselves in love to the world, to others, and ultimately to God.

Third, once the Mystic discovers in his own deep inner brokenness an intimacy with Christ who is eucharistically broken, poured out, and given for all, then the Mystic's celibate priesthood becomes capable of flowing out of deeper waters. Now the priest notices the desire and the capacity to bring others into a sacred encounter with Love at the core of their own brokenness, which is what the Eucharist is meant to be for all Christian men and women. Leading others to that sacred encounter comes from a more profound level of self-giving in priestly celibacy; it is *mystical generativity*, which comes from communion with the Presence of Love in one's center of being. As already noted, a priest's mysticism begins with his prayerful entrance through silence into his own deep center that leads him to experience a communion with Christ that provides what no other relationship, no other pursuit, no other achievement, no other blessing, no other noble grasp for what is good in life could ever offer.

The biblical theologian Gerhard Lohfink sees a paradigmatic understanding of celibacy in Jesus' very brief parables about the pearl of great price and the buried treasure (see Matt 13:44-46). Lohfink maintains that these parables are autobiographical, arising out of Jesus' own discovery of what the kingdom of God is for him:

> It is only in this context that Jesus' celibacy is comprehensible. If Jesus remained unmarried it was not because he despised sexuality or had a false attitude toward human physicality but simply because what had happened to him was like what he tells of in the parable of the hidden treasure and the precious pearl: he was seized and overpowered by the bliss of the reign of God—and not a reign that was coming some time in the future, but one that was beginning already, that one could already gain, that one could already cash in and deal with today.[14]

What Jesus has found in his relationship with God, the celibate priest in turn finds in Jesus Christ. Christ becomes "the pearl of great price,"

14. Gerhard Lohfink, *Jesus of Nazareth: What He Wanted, Who He Was* (Collegeville, MN: Liturgical Press, 2012), 236.

which is everything that God's love offers to broken human beings; it is everything for which the priest has always been looking but now discovers only through his silent entrance into the inner Presence of Love.

In his poem "The Truelove," David Whyte reflects on the powerful encounter between Jesus and Simon Peter as Jesus walks on turbulent waters toward him and the others in the boat, inviting Simon to step out onto the water with him. The poet's words capture the depth of love that can be found in the celibacy of the Mystic:

> There is a faith in loving fiercely
> the one who is rightfully yours,
> especially if you have
> waited years and especially
> if part of you never believed
> you could deserve this
> loved and beckoning hand
> held out to you this way.
>
> I am thinking of faith now
> and the testaments of loneliness
> and what we feel we are
> worthy of in this world.
>
> Years ago in the Hebrides,
> I remember an old man
> who walked every morning
> on the grey stones
> to the shore of baying seals,
>
> who would press his hat
> to his chest in the blustering
> salt wind and say his prayer
> to the turbulent Jesus
> hidden in the water,
>
> and I think of the story
> of the storm and everyone
> waking and seeing
> the distant,
> yet familiar figure,

far across the water
calling to them,

and how we are all
waiting for that
abrupt waking,
and that calling,
and that moment
we have to say *yes*,
except, it will
not come so grandly,
so Biblically,
but more subtly
and intimately, in the face
of the one you know
you have to love,

So that when
we finally step out of the boat
toward them, we find
everything holds
us, and everything confirms
our courage, and if you wanted
to drown you could,
but you don't,
because finally
after all this struggle
and all these years,
you don't want to any more,
you've simply had enough
of drowning,
and you want to live and you
want to love and you will
walk across any territory
and any darkness,
however fluid and however
dangerous, to take the
one hand you know
belongs in yours.[15]

15. David Whyte, *River Flow* (Langley, WA: Many Rivers Press, 2006), 198–200.

The beckoning hand of Christ calls us as Mystics to get out of the boat of constant doing and exclusively discursive prayer in order to step into the seemingly dangerous deeper waters of silent prayer. In these deeper waters, which our distractions and inner chatter can make seem like dangerous turbulence at first, are where we take the hand of Christ to discover what Christ has always *longed* to be for us and what we had always deeply wanted Christ to be but never allowed ourselves to discover because we were afraid to step into those waters. Once we do, we find that all that Christ is for us in our brokenness holds us and sustains us.

As priests, this encounter also allows us to hold out our hand to others in their brokenness. Once a priest experiences in his celibacy the fullness of all that Christ and only Christ can be for him in his fractured narrative in life, then an impetus arises in the priest to draw others to that same experience of life-giving, fulfilling communion with Christ. In seeking to be a Humble Mystic in Christ, the ordained Hero and Servant begins to discover a sacred way of offering his wounded self in Christ "for many," all of whom are themselves wounded. This is a further eucharistic dimension of celibacy: the celibate priest, joined to Christ's complete self-giving, leads others to a deeper experience of communion with Christ whom they now recognize as their True Love for their True Selves in their own fractured narratives in life.

At this point in a priest's spiritual biography, his mystical generativity can see what is wounded and fractured in others as very, very sacred since he has begun to look at himself from this lens. Furthermore, the priest begins to discover ways to be with others in their brokenness, much of which the priest cannot rid from their lives. While he can absolve the sins of others that arise from what is misguided and mistaken within them, most of the effects of the broken human condition perdure, yet they can be redeemed by being drawn into communion with Christ. This is what the priest's generativity does: it draws people to connect with Christ in their own fractured lives so that a grace-filled abundance in life can emerge from their brokenness. Because the Mystic has humbly discovered by now that human brokenness does not disappear, he continues to embrace people in theirs, each time embodying the True Love beckoning them. Sometimes this will mean that the priest can only bring the brokenness of others into his silent prayer and give it to Christ, again and again and again. Moreover, the Mystic will also draw what is tragic and shattered within the larger world into this silent surrender to what only the power of Christ's love can do.

Through mystical generativity a priest gives his own broken self to his people in a new way through his preaching, celebration of sacraments, and pastoral ministry. He might be doing the very same things he has always done, but a transparency develops that allows his inner life to help God's People see the sacredness of their murky, sometimes turbulent, sometimes peaceful inner lives; in short, the priest's inner life becomes a font of grace that helps others discover amazing intimacy with Christ in their own inner lives. For instance, the Mystic-in-Christ has less need to moralize in his preaching or always to instruct people on what they must live and instead can invite people to consider a way of engaging the presence of Christ in their prayer and pondering, letting Christ lead them to what they need to realize, experience, or do. The Mystic-in-Christ is not so obsessed with achieving only observable, measurable outcomes within his place of ministry but guides people in their prayerful pondering as a community about the outcomes, measurable or not, to which the Spirit of Christ might be directing them. Most likely this will mean having to teach the people how to pray, ponder, and discern.

When it comes to celebrating the sacraments, the Mystic-in-Christ will reflect an engaging communion with the One who is at the center of the celebration, the One who is beckoning those receiving sacraments to open up to what Christ deeply desires to be for them. The Mystic-in-Christ names clearly, with conviction and credibility, what the sacramental encounter with Christ will bring to a person's life, both one's inner life and one's outer life. And in every form of ministry, the Mystic priest can inspire God's People to recognize, as he has, that everyone they encounter is a broken human being and that the brokenness of others is as sacred as one's own. Furthermore, he will inspire others to give themselves as Mystics-in-Christ to a broken world. Appropriately, he will be able to show others how in their own lives they can find the deeper current that draws them to do this. This is the generativity of celibacy at its best.

For this kind of *mystical generativity* to be sustained, however, the priest will need to return to his practice of silence each day. Only the silence can allow all that the priest celebrates in the Eucharist, lives as a celibate, and offers in pastoral ministry to emerge from the Love that is Jesus Christ. Only the silence can evoke from within the priest the heroic energy to do nobly what can seem quite daunting to do—to enter one's wounds but now to do it out of a deep communion with Christ. Only the silence can draw from the steadfast energy inside a priest to be a faithful servant alongside Christ in day-to-day ministry; only now that steadfastness comes from an inner yoke that connects the priest's True Self to Christ. Finally, only the silence can allow the Mystic to find his True Love deep inside of him and to give himself as that Love to others. The ordained man who habitually enters stillness allows everything about himself to become so wonderfully claimed by Christ that now he lives in Christ. In this way, the eucharistic words, "This is my body given for you; this is the cup of my blood poured out for you," are now recognized as bringing forth both the complete self-offering of Christ and also the priest. This is when the spiritual biography of a priest has truly put out into the deep waters.

✛ CHAPTER FOUR

The Archetypes in the "Ark-of-Types"

The flood continued for forty days on the earth; and the waters increased, and bore up the ark, and it rose high above the earth. The waters swelled and increased greatly on the earth; and the ark floated on the face of the waters. . . . Only Noah was left, and those that were with him in the ark.
—Genesis 7:17-18, 23

The Vessel of Communion with Others

The Hebrew word for the ark built by Noah is *tebah*, which is also the word for the papyrus basket into which the infant Moses is placed in the Nile River by his mother. These passages teach us that the *tebah* is the vessel of God's protection and care for those who are to be agents of God's redemptive work in the world.[1] The *tebah* is a vessel in which people are led securely by God through the sometimes turbulent and often deep waters of grace that flood their lives and can also on occasion seem overwhelming. In the story of Noah, when God decides to cleanse the world of its sinfulness and refashion his creation, God directs Noah to build a sacred vessel in which God would shelter and

---

1. The link between the vessel of Noah and the vessel of Moses is well documented in biblical commentaries. For their symbolism as vessels of God's providence and care, see Thomas Joseph White, *Exodus*, vol. 2 in the *Brazos Theological Commentary on the Bible* (Grand Rapids, MI: Brazos Press, 2016), 32–33. See also Carol Meyers, *Exodus*, vol. 2 of *The New Cambridge Bible Commentary* (New York: Cambridge University Press, 2005), 43.

hold on to those who will continue the covenant with him. When the floods come, Noah is not meant to enter that ark alone; otherwise the human species and the animal kingdom would not continue. His wife, his three sons, and their wives all enter into the ark with Noah, along with "every wild animal of every kind, and all domestic animals of every kind, and every creeping thing that creeps on the earth, and every bird of every kind" (Gen 7:14). Thus, when the torrential rains fall, sheltered in the safety of that vessel are different generations of faith and devotion who were to care for what God had brought to life.

In the center of the vessel there is the abiding faithfulness and mysticism of the righteous man Noah, "who walked with God" (Gen 6:9). Surely he and his wife exhibited the wise energy of having navigated many years of fidelity to God. As the book of Genesis relates, "Noah was six hundred years old when the flood of waters came on the earth" (Gen 7:6); whether a literal or symbolic number, surely that signifies a long journey of faith. Also in the ark, however, are the youthful exuberance and vigor of Shem, Ham, and Japheth, whose valiant energy was needed in order to build the ark in the first place, then courageously round up the animals both wild and tame. After this heroic feat, with a steadfastness needed for the long haul, this younger generation is to help care for all the animals in the ark until the waters receded from the earth. More important, these sons and their wives are to produce children after the flood to continue the progeny of Noah that ultimately will become the Chosen People of God. Thus, all the different human archetypal energies are preserved in that ark, and there with each other, they are protected by God.

The narrative of Noah and his family suggests that the *tebah* into which God calls us is never meant to be a solitary vessel that we enter alone. (Even in the story of Moses, his sister is always nearby as he floats down the Nile in his papyrus basket [Exod 2:4]; she is God's protection in the water with Moses.[2]) While anyone's spiritual journey definitely includes moments of aloneness, solitary prayer and pondering, and the privacy of one's deep interiority, what God seeks to offer the world in and through each spiritual person is not meant to be achieved by solo practitioners of ministry. Nor is the ark of God's grace that safeguards

2. White, *Exodus*, 32.

people's lives in and through priestly ministry meant to be a vessel with only one priestly archetype, exclusive of those exhibiting different archetypal energy. In order for priesthood to be effectively the means of God's providential care for his people, the Heroes, the Servants, and the Mystics need to be in the ark together; the priesthood needs to be an "ark-of-types." Therefore, within each presbyterate of each local church and within each religious order, men at all stages of archetypal energy and all valid expressions of that energy need to be in communion with each other. From my perspective, this is one of the key elements in the theological notion of the *presbyterium* that was rediscovered by Vatican II but has lain dormant since the council, still to be explored with greater depth both theologically and spiritually.

When a man is ordained a priest, he is ordained into a presbyterate—not only the universal order of the ministerial priesthood in the church, but also the specific *presbyterium* of a priest's local church or religious community. In *Lumen Gentium* (Dogmatic Constitution on the Church), the fathers of Vatican II state: "In virtue of their sacred ordination and of their common mission, all priests are united together by bonds of intimate brotherhood. This should manifest itself in mutual help, spiritual or temporal, pastoral or personal, spontaneously and freely given in reunions and togetherness in life, work and charity" (LG 28).[3] They continue: "Since the human race today is tending more and more towards civil, economic and social unity, it is all the more necessary that priests should unite their efforts and combine their resources under the leadership of the bishops and the Supreme Pontiff and thus eliminate division and dissension in every shape or form, so that all humanity may be led into the unity of the family of God" (LG 28). The Second Vatican Council has taught that the presbyterate needs to become a true brotherhood so that it can embody the very state of communion into which all the People of God are drawn. A fractured or fractious presbyterate cannot do this.

The pivotal declaration on the *presbyterium* within each local church is offered by Vatican II's *Presbyterorum Ordinis* (Decree on the

3. All quotations from the Second Vatican Council are taken from *Vatican Council II: Constitutions, Decrees, Declarations; The Basic Sixteen Documents*, ed. Austin Flannery (Collegeville, MN: Liturgical Press, 2014).

Ministry and Life of Priests), issued near the end of the council in 1965. The document states:

> All priests, who are constituted in the order of priesthood by the sacrament of order, are bound together by an intimate sacramental brotherhood; but in a special way they form one priestly body in the diocese to which they are attached under their own bishop. For even though they may be assigned different duties, yet for their people they fulfill the one priestly service. Indeed all priests are sent to cooperate in the same work. This is true whether the ministry they exercise be parochial or supra-parochial. . . . They all contribute to the same purpose, namely the building up of the body of Christ, and this, especially in our times, demands many kinds of duties and fresh adaptations.
>
> For this reason it is of great importance that all priests, whether diocesan or regular, should help each other, so that they may be fellow-workers in the service of truth. . . . So priests are all united with their brother priests by the bond of charity, prayer, and total cooperation. In this way is made manifest the consummation of that unity which Christ wished for his own, that the world might know that the Son had been sent by the Father. (PO 8)

Then, in a very direct statement that has much sage advice to offer the different generations of priests, the council fathers insist:

> From this it follows that older priests should sincerely accept younger priests as brothers and help them in facing the first tasks and responsibilities of their ministry. They should make an effort also to understand their outlook even though it may be different from their own, and should give kindly encouragement to their projects. Young priests for their part are to respect the age and experience of their elders; they ought to consult with them on matters concerning the care of souls and willingly co-operate with them.
>
> Under the influence of the spirit of brotherhood priests should not forget hospitality, and should cultivate kindness and the sharing of goods. (PO 8)

The council fathers continue with a strong admonition for priests to seek ways of living in common, meeting regularly in prayer and fraternity, and reaching out to priests experiencing difficulty or who are in trouble (PO 8).

The nature of communion among priests described above by *Presbyterorum Ordinis* still remains a distant reality in many, if not most, presbyterates. Furthermore, among many diocesan priests who experience a growing disconnect from other priests of different generations or ideologies, there is a tendency to retreat into a fiercely protected individualism or a very circumscribed circle of priest friends. For them the notion of the *presbyterium* described by Vatican II is something about which they are very disinterested. Yet a presbyterate without deep communion leads to a weakened exercise of priesthood. Admittedly, however, achieving communion among the members of a local *presbyterium* can be quite challenging.

A Personal Reflection and Challenge

One year for Holy Week I was privileged to make a pilgrimage to the Holy Land. I met a colleague over there who was finishing a sabbatical in Jerusalem and knew his way around the Holy Land quite well. When we traveled north of Jerusalem to the Sea of Tiberias, I found the scenery breathtaking and very conducive to prayer and pondering. One morning, while I was sitting and praying by the sea, my gaze became fixed on a fisherman's boat on the shoreline. Instantly the whole narrative of Christ's call of the first disciples (Luke 5:1-7) came to me. As I pondered that biblical story and imagined the whole scene playing out in front of me, I realized that I was sitting near the very sacred waters of the first yes to Christ by those who would minister in his name. Then I became filled with gratitude and admiration for those seminarians with whom I was privileged to accompany in their own yes to Christ. I offered my own prayers of thanks to God for his continued inspiration of me through these younger men. And I offered prayers of petition that God, who had begun the marvelously good work in them, would bring it to fulfillment. After a long time sitting on the shoreline of Tiberias that wonderful morning looking on a fisherman's boat, it dawned on me that in those waters in front of me was a whole lineage of yeses from Heroes, Servants, and Mystics who responded to Christ's call for more than two thousand years. As my prayer continued I imagined Christ down at the shoreline, asking me to join him in the boat. When I walked to the boat, Jesus stepped aside and in the boat were all the wonderful seminarians and priests who had been a part of my prayer all morning. I felt so blessed to have been drawn into their company in my own imperfect yes to Christ.

Several weeks after that moment in the Holy Land I was on my annual retreat. During prayer one day that whole scene on the shore of the Sea of Tiberias came rushing back to me, and with it all of my feelings of admiration for the younger men in the seminary as well as for all the priests who had inspired me over the years. Again, the prayer brought me a sense of truly being graced by Christ in the call to priesthood. When I returned to the scene again later in prayer on that retreat (Ignatius of Loyola always stresses the importance of *repetitio* in our prayer), a very different experience occurred. This time in my imaginative pondering of the scene, Jesus is sitting next to me on the shoreline. He turns to me and thanks me for my years as a priest, but then he indicates that I have further to go in my yes to him; so he asks me to join him in the boat. Jesus walks down to the boat and stands in front of it and again asks me to join him. As I approach the boat Jesus steps aside and this time in the boat are priests that I have struggled with greatly: men whose perspectives, priorities, and personalities have really grated on me. They are what I have labeled in my journal as the "Difficult Others," which, I am sure, would be an apt label for me in their journals. Of course, in my imagined scene I recoil from Jesus' invitation, though I am still drawn to being with him. Finally, Jesus says to me, "Scott, in order to be in the boat with me, you have to also be in the boat with them. Communion with me is communion with them." Yikes! That was all I could muster inside of me as a response at that moment. As my retreat continued and as my praying into that scene was repeated over and over again, it became clear to me that Jesus was asking me to enter into a deeper stage of my yes to his call to priesthood. I needed to enter into that place of communion with Christ in my own brokenness where I could find a genuine sense of being in communion with the brokenness in the "Difficult Others," including the "Difficult Other Priests" in my life, who will always be in my life in one form or another.

Within the archetypal energy of the Mystic in Christ is the calling and capacity to bring that sense of communion into a priest's own presbyterate. When a priest reaches that place of inner communion with Christ in his brokenness, he discovers a new way of being with others in their brokenness, including other priests who seem so different from himself. But as my own spiritual biography evidences, this is much easier said than done; it is a lofty virtue that is very hard to live.

It is no secret that a great divide has opened up within presbyterates in the last few decades. At one time it was labeled the "Vatican II priests" versus the "John Paul II priests," and to some extent that might still hold. There is also more recently, however, a divide between those who have been caught up in "the Francis effect" and those exhibiting "Benedict loyalty." Regardless of how we label it, the divide among priests is as palpable as it is painful. It is probably not a new phenomenon in the history of priesthood, but it has become more pronounced because it is reflecting and fueled by the growing ideological divides within our society, especially along political lines. Our culture increasingly exhibits a hostile manner of discourse that vilifies one's opponent. In addition, the so-called liturgy wars of the 1990s exacerbated the toxicity of ideological differences among priests. On one side were those excited by a more expansive use of inculturation and the expanded role of the laity within the liturgy, and so they sought to craft a liturgical experience that bridged worship and daily life. On the other side were those who felt liturgy had lost its sacredness, and so they wanted to restore the sense of transcendence in the Mass that induced awe and wonder within the participants who prayerfully watched what the priest enacted. The result was a stark contrast between subgroups within a local presbyterate, and that contrast has often created animosity. The members of one group have tended to see those in other groups as "Difficult Others," persons who were not easy to be with and around whom one needed to be guarded. For each of us the "Difficult Other Priest" comes in different forms, even beyond that of liturgical issues. It might also be one who expresses a different ecclesiology, one who wears different clerical dress, one who sees priesthood differently than we do, one who lives a different lifestyle, one with different priorities in ministry, one who has a very different personality, one who likes a different pope. The list could go on and on.

The Mystic in Christ begins to see that underneath all the differences there is something strikingly the same—a very broken human being whose brokenness is the place of communion with Christ. You and I may never know the nature of another person's brokenness. The other person, including the "Difficult Other Priest," may not even yet really know the nature of his own brokenness. He may be hiding from it, running from it, or trying to compensate for it. Perhaps he does recognize it and, like the rest of us, is making some efforts to integrate his brokenness into his self-understanding, his exercise of priestly ministry, and his relationship with Christ but still has a long way to go. Rest assured, however, no matter where the "Difficult Other Priest" is in this process, his brokenness is there. And so is our own.

The Importance of a Will to Communion

When the Mystic priest enters into communion with Christ in his own brokenness, what grows within him is what I call a "will to communion," that is, a deep desire to be a person who more often than not seeks unity rather than division, creates a comfortable setting for others rather than a tense or hostile environment, and bears others' flaws and failings with compassion and equanimity rather than judgment and hostility. Granted, all of this is easier to recognize as an important quality to be developed than it is a disposition that is actually lived. Nevertheless, I consider having this "will to communion" to be an essential virtue in our current societal ethos of open hostility and the church's propensity toward divisiveness.[4]

The will to communion is exercised when we stay at the table with each other. We see the origins of this in Jesus' own table fellowship. For instance, Jesus dines at the home of Simon the Pharisee (Luke 7:36-50) even though Luke has already told us that "the Pharisees and the lawyers rejected God's purpose for themselves" (Luke 7:30) and even though Simon cannot understand or accept Christ's mission of mercy when he forgives the sinful woman who has also approached the table (Luke 7:37, 48). In all accounts of the Lord's Supper, Jesus sits at table with the one he knows will betray him. John's account even goes so far as to mention that Jesus breaks bread with Judas (John 13:26). Furthermore, Jesus knowingly dines with the one who will deny him (Luke 22:34).

---

4. See my "The Will to Communion as a Theological and Ministerial Virtue," *New Theology Review* 21 (2008): 60–69.

The powerful example of Jesus remaining in table fellowship even with those who oppose him, reject him, or disappoint him must have remained seared in the memory of the apostles. When the early church began to experience the first signs of divisiveness that threatened their unity, this sense of table fellowship became part of the apostles' solution. This can be seen at the Council of Jerusalem (see Acts 15:1-29). The nascent church was already threatened by schism because of the difficulty of knowing how to handle the situation of Gentile converts to Christianity: Should they be made to also adhere to the tenets of the Torah as the Jewish Christians were doing? Paul and Barnabas raised objections to making the Gentiles comply with the Torah; believers from the pharisaic party wanted absolute adherence.[5]

The solution that is arrived at and announced by James is interesting. The apostle declares that the Gentile converts merely need to follow the precepts of the Torah that demand they "abstain only from things polluted by idols and from fornication and from whatever has been strangled and from blood" (Acts 15:20). As Luke Timothy Johnson points out, all of these conditions are tenets from the Levitical code of ritual purity and the necessary conditions for table fellowship. Hence James' decision is meant to be a reconciling measure that would allow Jewish Christians to be at table with Gentile Christians because the Gentile Christians would not be engaging in practices of radical disharmony with the Jewish notion of table fellowship.[6] Therefore, the decision agreed to by the Council of Jerusalem was a measure to keep communion—to keep the followers of Christ at table with one another.

As a *presbyterium*, we can do no other than that; it is incumbent on us as priests to stay at the table with one another, including with those who are "Different Others" and "Difficult Others." This means not only the table of the Eucharist but also the table of discussion, the table of fellowship on days of recollection or other priest gatherings, the meeting table for when priests serve on committees together, the table of cooperation with parish and diocesan efforts at fulfilling the church's mission, and the dinner table in the rectory. But it also means being with each other at the table of prayer in silence, the interior table of

5. See Luke Timothy Johnson, *The Acts of the Apostles*, Sacra Pagina 5, ed. Daniel J. Harrington (Collegeville, MN: Liturgical Press, 1992), 73.
6. Ibid.

intimacy with Christ, and the table of the will to communion that comes from the spiritual recognition that Christ loves us deeply in our own brokenness and therefore loves every priest in his own brokenness.[7]

But as with the apostles at the Council of Jerusalem so too with us: developing a will to communion is difficult. We all know priests who refuse to come to priest gatherings, who never attend priestly ordinations, and who absent themselves from cooperative efforts with other priests. These are men who are broken like the rest of us but who have yet to discover their inner communion with Christ in their brokenness and how that communion binds them to all others, including other priests. The will to communion with other priests has to come from our own interior communion with Christ who dwells within our priestly brokenness, that is, inside what can make us a "Different Other" or a "Difficult Other" to fellow priests. It is only through the power of Christ who dwells within us that we can stay at the table with those with whom we struggle the most or who may struggle greatly with us.

The Nature of Communion

The deep layers of communion come out of the very heart of God as revealed in Jesus Christ. On the night before he dies, Jesus, while at table with his disciples, prays:

> Holy Father,
> protect them in your name
> that you have given me,
> so that they may be one, as we are one. . . .
> I ask not only on behalf of these,
> but also on behalf of those who will believe in me
> through their word,
> that they may all be one.
> As you, Father, are in me and I am in you,

7. Of course, this will to communion ought to be extended not only to other priests; it is a virtue that priests need to exhibit with all other people within the church as well as people of all faiths and walks of life. Additionally, it is a virtue that priests need to cultivate in the people they serve through their preaching and their evident manner of dealing with the "Different Others" and "Difficult Others" within their pastoral practice. I explore this aspect of the will to communion more fully in my article cited earlier in this chapter.

may they also be in us,
so that the world may believe that you have sent me.
The glory that you have given me
I have given them,
so that they may be one, as we are one,
I in them and you in me,
that they may become completely one,
so that the world may know that you have sent me
and have loved them even as you have loved me. (John 17:11, 20-23)

This prayer of Christ, which is the final prayer of Christ uttered aloud before he dies, is a deep desire for communion in the world; for it is only through lived communion that the world will recognize and believe in the Communion that is God and then experience the ultimate expression of that Communion—God's love. Therefore, the Communion that is God the Trinity defines the communion at our deepest core, and it impels us to become men of communion as priests.

In *Pastores Dabo Vobis*, St. John Paul II considers the priest to be essentially a "man of communion." He writes:

> In order that his ministry may be humanly as credible and acceptable as possible, it is important that the priest should mold his human personality in such a way that it becomes a bridge and not an obstacle for others in their meeting with Jesus Christ the Redeemer of humanity. It is necessary that, following the example of Jesus who "knew what was in humanity" (Jn. 2:25; cf. 8:3-11), the priest should be able to know the depths of the human heart, to perceive difficulties and problems, to make meeting and dialogue easy, to create trust and cooperation, to express serene and objective judgments.
>
> Of special importance is the capacity to relate to others. This is truly fundamental for a person who is called to be responsible for a community and to be a "man of communion." This demands that the priest not be arrogant, or quarrelsome, but affable, hospitable, sincere in his words and heart, prudent and discreet, generous and ready to serve, capable of opening himself to clear and brotherly relationships and of encouraging the same in others, and quick to understand, forgive and console (cf. 1 Tm. 3:1-5; Ti. 1:7-9).[8]

8. Pope John Paul II, *Pastores Dabo Vobis*, Postsynodal Apostolic Exhortation, no. 43.

In recent years Pope Francis has embodied an amazing drive and will to communion. His call for us to be a church of mercy is a summons to transform distance, divisiveness, and hostility into compassionate communion. Pope Francis writes in *Evangelii Gaudium*:

> Differences between persons and communities can sometimes prove uncomfortable, but the Holy Spirit, who is the source of that diversity, can bring forth something good from all things and turn it into an attractive means of evangelization. Diversity must always be reconciled by the help of the Holy Spirit; he alone can raise up diversity, plurality and multiplicity while at the same time bringing about unity. When we, for our part, aspire to diversity, we become self-enclosed, exclusive and divisive; similarly, whenever we attempt to create unity on the basis of human calculations, we end up imposing a monolithic uniformity. This is not helpful for the Church's mission.[9]

The words of Pope Francis reinforce the need for a priest to examine not only his capacity to be a man of communion but even if he possesses a "will to communion."

Archetypal Energies as a Place of Communion

The spiritual biography that has been outlined in this book has offered a schema of the different stages of priestly spirituality based on the shifts that come from three major archetypal energies that arise from deep within priests. Each of these archetypes is sacred and necessary for priestly life and ministry, yet it is clear that each might be expressed in different ways in different generations of priesthood and eras of the church. As archetypes, they arise from the most inner depths of the soul of the man who is ordained. Therefore, they are not mere cultural phenomena that come and go; nor are they mere historical expressions of priesthood in a timebound period of church history. Furthermore, they are not forms of energy that are present in some priests but not in others. As archetypes, they arise from deep within each priest who truly desires to develop a mature and integrated spiritual life. Also, it is important to remember that each of the three archetypes is present

---

9. Pope Francis, *Evangelii Gaudium* (Washington, DC: USCCB, 2013), no. 131.

with the other two, so no archetype is ever really lost as a priest's narrative unfolds over time. Instead, each is sublated into the next stage; that is, each prior archetype becomes something more than it previously was as a priest's spiritual narrative advances to greater depth. Therefore, by recalling one's own progression and place within these stages, any priest who has a will to communion ought to be able to find some level of connection with any other priest who is at any stage. What this means is that the communion potentially existing within the ark-of-types among priests needs to be (and *can* be) built because that ark-of-types exists within each priest who has taken seriously his own inner life. In short, the interior ark-of-types in each *one* can generate the interrelational ark-of-types among the *many*.

From that perspective, each priest can recognize that, while his expression of the Hero for Christ might be very different ecclesiologically or liturgically from someone else's, it is the same energy. For instance, one Hero-for-Christ priest, assuming that he is being rather genuine, might prefer to celebrate very traditional liturgy with incense and bells and fiddle-back vestments because he wants to save people from the ravages of a secular world and he earnestly believes that a more transcendent sense of liturgy could help with that. On the other hand, another Hero-for-Christ priest, also assuming him to be rather genuine, might be interested in conducting service trips with his parishioners and engaging them in social advocacy work because he ardently believes the church needs to save people from the injustices of the world that wound the human soul. It is the same energy, just different expressions. Keep in mind that neither priest would have purely genuine motives, for no one does. Both priests, however, on some level, are directing their energy toward brokenness out in the world in front of them, and they are trying to do something for Christ in that place of brokenness. In the end, these distinctions between the priests serve only to demonstrate that heroes come in different forms; heroes seek to rescue people from different dangers. Furthermore, any priest who has moved into the next stages of Servant with Christ or Mystic in Christ can recognize himself in some expression of that earlier stage of Hero for Christ. It is from that recognition of one's own perduring heroic archetypal energy deep inside that the capacity for communion arises. This is an example of where the interior ark-of-types becomes operative within a priest's efforts to enter the ark-of-types among priests.

Furthermore, in the Servant-with-Christ stage, a priest's archetypal energy now comes from a deeper place of prayer where Christ's companionship at his side sustains him through the difficult and dark hours of priestly life and ministry. What one priest struggles with at this stage, however, might be very different from that with which another priest struggles. And the manner in which one priest feels closer to Christ—more yoked to Christ—might be very distinct from the way other priests do. For instance, a priest struggling with being an effective preacher might spend more time visiting hospitals because that makes him feel more effective as a priest and more closely connected to Christ. He will, however, have to discover Christ's companionship in his struggles with preaching; Christ the Teacher will need to be his guide. Another priest who struggles with administrative duties might find consolation in spending more time on preparing his homilies because he feels most effective as a priest in that ministry. His prayer will need to lead him to Christ's companionship in his leadership and administrative roles; Christ the Shepherd of the Flock will need to be his mentor. If both priests, who might struggle with each other's styles and emphases, could recognize that the other one is also seeking to be with Christ in the midst of his struggles in priesthood, then a sense of communion could arise between them.

The point of all of these examples is that as priests we need to get beyond seeing our differences on the outside to recognizing our communion with each other in Christ on the inside, within the deep waters of priestly spirituality. Different emphases in priestly life and ministry, different styles, different interests, different personalities, different preferences, different theologies can actually be coming from the very same flow of archetypal energy inside all priests. When a priest struggles to find communion with another priest, especially the "Difficult Other Priest," then he needs to hear the call of the Mystic inside of him who is seeking to draw him deeper into his own brokenness to a powerful level of communion with Christ who dwells within him. Martin Laird offers this assessment: "The indwelling presence of Christ is not only the core of human identity, but also something (a something that's not a thing) that resolves dualities, which, at more superficial levels of awareness, appear to be opposites."[10]

10. Laird, *Into the Silent Land*, 13.

Richard Rohr recognizes the danger of dualities that linger within the spiritual life. He claims that the movement away from dualistic thinking is the accomplishment in grace of those in the second half of life who have done their inner work, that is, those who have been operating for a long time as Servants and have begun to discover their inner Mystic. Before that happens, Rohr claims that the dualistic mind-set that predominates in persons suffers from the "seven Cs of delusion" operating within it: "it compares, it competes, it conflicts, it conspires, it condemns, it cancels out any contrary evidence, and it then crucifies with impunity."[11] Dualistic thinking is so prevalent in our culture; it rears its ugly head as divisiveness, the need to cast blame on others, and the lack of civil discourse. Within the spiritual biography of priests, the Noble Hero for Christ is particularly susceptible to this manner of thinking because it is difficult for one who is so powerfully energized and focused on a valiant purpose to feel united with those who are not driven by the same motives or a like-minded assessment of the church's role in the world and the priest's role in the church. So too can the Faithful Servant with Christ be caught up in dualistic thinking when he gives priority to certain elements of the day-to-day exercise of priestly ministry but then can be dismissive of what other priests are prioritizing. Even the Mystic in Christ can find at times that within his engagement of silence the "mental chatter" that keeps distracting him can include resentment toward other priests or other styles of priesthood. The more he enters into the silence to discover the powerful oneness he has with Christ in his brokenness, however, then the more he moves beyond the "seven Cs" of delusion and divisiveness.

Even among those who do take prayer seriously, there will be mistakes, character flaws, and sin because each priest is a broken person. Nevertheless, the important efforts to move beyond dualistic thinking in order to discover communion with all others does not mean that one should ignore the misdeeds of other priests or blithely dismiss them because "we are all broken." That common brokenness is an invitation to care for other priests, not an exemption from challenging them in a thoughtful but firm manner. The fractured narrative of all priests beckons them to go always deeper into prayer and discover

---

11. Richard Rohr, *Falling Upward: A Spirituality of the Two Halves of Life* (San Francisco: Jossey-Bass, 2011), 147.

communion with Christ in their woundedness and communion with every priest in Christ. Likewise, when one priest notices something about another priest that might need to be challenged, if he first recognizes his communion with that other priest, then the challenge he would offer would come from a genuine sense of compassion and not an emotional rush of derision. This would be "fraternal correction" at its best, though it does not guarantee it will work. Unfortunately, ministerial malpractice will always be a reality, especially from those who do not take the spiritual life seriously.

Furthermore, despite all of our efforts at maintaining a healthy prayer life, it is important to recognize that all archetypes have their shadow side to them. A Hero's self-assuredness about his noble efforts can render him a narcissist or, when frustrated or opposed, a bully. A Servant, who has faithfully labored with Christ for a long time, can begin to expect due recompense for all that he has done and, because of that, devolve into an entitled child. Even the Mystic can mistakenly recede into the idleness or reticence of the disinterested spectator. Therefore, it is incumbent on every priest that, no matter what stage of archetypal energy he is living from, he not allow his spiritual archetype to run on automatic pilot; being a Hero or Servant or Mystic will always need to be formed and nourished by a committed prayer life.

The Return to the Ark

This chapter began with the image of Noah and his wife, wisdom figures to be sure, needing their younger sons and their wives in the ark with them in order to navigate successfully the torrential storm that was flooding the earth and to bring about efficaciously the saving plan of God. This image suggests that the ark is a vessel of communion that holds within it all the archetypes of those who live their lives in service of God's calling; in short, the vessel is an "ark-of-types."

In summary, this vessel is important for navigating the deeper waters of priestly spirituality for two main reasons. First of all, as already stated, the ark-of-types can exist within each priest. Recall one of the key operative principles in the spiritual biography of priests: no previous archetypal energy is lost, but rather each is sublated into the next stage. This means that the Hero, the Servant, and the Mystic must always be together within each priest. While it is true that one archetype will exert more influence than the others, appropriate to the stage of spiritual development a priest is in, the other two will still have their sway. For instance, when the priest operates out of the predominantly Hero-for-Christ energy inside of him, the Servant will provide the perseverance to keep going in the midst of difficult moments of ministry when there are not easily recognizable positive results from what the Hero is doing. Furthermore, the Mystic will constantly beckon the Hero to go deeper into prayer and eventually to discover the sacredness of his own fractured and wounded life.

When a priest moves into the Servant-with-Christ stage of his spiritual biography, the Hero will still provide the capacity to face with courage the daunting moments (e.g., being called to the emergency room in the middle of the night) or to move out of one's comfort zones in the exercise of pastoral ministry. In addition, the Mystic, as in the previous stage, will continue to beckon the priest to go deeper into his interior life and discover the companionship of Christ in his brokenness.

As a priest discovers the level of being a Mystic in Christ in his spiritual life, the previous archetypes still provide needed energy boosts. As before, the Hero continues to provide the impetus to meet head-on the very trying and difficult moments in ministry. It is also the Hero who allows the now seasoned and experienced priest to venture out with new ideas and new approaches to the constant needs of the church. The Servant is the source of stick-to-itiveness after many years of long days and limited results in ministry.

A second reason for the importance of the priestly ark-of-types that was developed in this chapter is that it can become a vessel of communion among the priests of a local church or religious community. The need for such a vessel of communion is so crucial at this moment in the history of priesthood, when the church has been flooded by the extremely painful revelations of decades of abhorrent and aberrant behavior by some priests and bishops. These revelations have added a whole new layer to the wound that lies within the brokenness of every priest. Now it is a collective wound that scars not only how others perceive the priesthood but also how priests "feel priesthood" within themselves. The Hero desperately wants to restore the shining image of the priesthood and make recompense for what other priests have perpetrated; the Servant becomes acutely aware of the need to be truly authentic in what he brings to others; and the Mystic begins to weep in his prayer because of all that has been lost and all who have been hurt by the perfidious behavior of brother priests. In addition, the collective wound festers when good and faithful priests are made subject to public ridicule, scorn, and antipathy because of how other people are processing their own pain and anger over what has transpired in the church.

For these reasons, the ark of priesthood is enduring a particularly virulent storm that threatens to flood priests' inner lives with shame, anger, hypersensitivity, vocational doubt, and listless commitment. This storm may also flood the hearts and minds of priests with the need to blame other priests for what has gone terribly wrong, to label other priests who are different from them as "suspicious," or to distance themselves from other priests altogether. More than ever, priests need to be in the ark with each other. They ought to recognize how much they need each other to weather the storm and to continue the saving mission of Jesus Christ. They ought to participate deliberately in the *presbyterium* of their local church and contribute fruitfully to the healing for which it yearns. Furthermore, they have to muster the heroic, steadfast, and deeply prayerful energy that dwells within them. As priests there is an amazing and grace-filled ark-of-types within us and among us.

✠ CHAPTER FIVE

The Archetypes in Initial and Ongoing Priestly Formation

> *In the day that the LORD God made the earth and the heavens, when no plant of the field was yet in the earth and no herb of that field had sprung up—for the LORD God had not caused it to rain upon the earth, and there was no one to till the ground; but a stream would rise from the earth, and water the whole face of the ground—then the LORD God formed man from the dust of the ground, and breathed into his nostrils the breath of life.*
> *—Genesis 2:4b-7a*

Navigating the Waters of Priestly Spirituality

Long before the study of physiology demonstrated that water constitutes the vast majority of the human body, the biblical accounts of creation revealed that water is an essential element of the sacred nature of the human person.[1] In the second account of creation, primeval waters have seeped into the ground, and from that muddy soil the first human being was formed and fashioned by God. Therefore, those primeval waters of God's creative care and energy are now deep within every human being, and they symbolically represent an inner place where each human creature encounters the tender love of the Creator.

---

1. Both accounts of creation in Genesis demonstrate this reality. Besides the passage from the second account of creation quoted above, water is present in the first account as God creates (cf. Gen 1:1-3).

This biblical symbolism makes clear that the deep waters of our spiritual lives form the very essence of who we are. At our core we are constituted by the water of life from God. To ignore or to minimize that reality threatens the very quality of our humanness. For a priest, it also diminishes the depth and effectiveness of his priestly identity. God, who crafted the *humanness* of each priest out of the living stream of the water of life, does the same with a man's *priesthood*. Thus, God calls the ordained man as both a human person and a priest to enter constantly into that inner stream in order for both his humanness and his priesthood to become fully alive.

That inner stream is characterized by shifting currents. Knowing how to navigate these shifting currents of the inner life is extremely important for the durability of priestly life and ministry. Seminarians, newly ordained men, and long-ordained priests need to be aware of the transformations that will happen inside of them, even as they remain faithful to their vocation and to the spiritual life. They ought to recognize that at their core is the water of life from which they were created, out of which they were called, and into which they are constantly summoned in prayer. This interior spring is their deep and intimate relationship with Christ, who configures them to his own priesthood, who beckons them onward in ministry and inward in prayer, and who empowers them to do awesome things for the People of God while discovering amazing grace in their deeply wounded self. Keeping these insights embedded within a man's consciousness is crucial in both the initial and ongoing stages of priestly formation. St. John Paul II states: "The formation of future priests, both diocesan and religious, and lifelong assiduous care for their personal sanctification in the ministry and for the constant updating of their pastoral commitment is considered by the Church one of the most demanding and important tasks for the future of the evangelization of humanity."[2]

This important task of evangelization requires that seminary formators instill in candidates for priesthood far-reaching and durable insight about the nature of spiritual growth and development. This means that formators are to prepare seminarians for the turbulent upheavals that lie ahead for them not just in ministry but also as they

2. Pope John Paul II, *Pastores Dabo Vobis* (PDV), Postsynodal Apostolic Exhortation, no. 2.

navigate the shifting currents within their spiritual biography. Likewise, bishops, clergy personnel directors, directors of continuing formation, and vicars for priests must help their priests be aware of how their spiritual lives and priestly energy will change over time, leading to periods of both desolation and consolation. Furthermore, they ought to keep their priests attentive to the shifting currents in the spiritual life. In short, those who oversee the continuing formation and well-being of the already ordained must be insistent that priests learn how to "put out into the deep water." They cannot be content only with overseeing the priests as practitioners of ministry; they must have assiduous concern for priests as pray-ers. What follows are some suggestions for the periods of both initial and ongoing priestly formation.

Part 1: An Archetypal Template for Seminary Formation

Welcome the Hero; Train the Servant; Uncover the Mystic

All that has been described in the previous chapters portrays a narrative within the life of a priest that is clearly spiritual but also a storyline that draws inexorably from his own human growth and development, pastoral experience, and intellectual training. Hence, the spiritual biography of priests is a chronicle of true integration of the four pillars of formation that begin but do not end with seminary training. When St. John Paul II spoke of these pillars in *Pastores Dabo Vobis*, he asserted: "Human maturity, and in particular affective maturity, requires a clear and strong training in freedom, which expresses itself in convinced and heartfelt obedience to the 'truth' of one's own being, to the 'meaning' of one's own existence, that is to the 'sincere gift of self' as the way and fundamental content of the authentic realization of self" (PDV 44). He then went on to say, "Human formation, when it is carried out in the context of an anthropology which is open to the full truth regarding the human person, leads to and finds its completion in spiritual formation" (PDV 45).

Because of St. John Paul's treatise on human and spiritual formation, along with what he offers on intellectual and pastoral formation, the fifth edition of the *Program for Priestly Formation* (PPF), issued by the United States Conference of Catholic Bishops in 2005, finally mentions all four pillars of priestly life for the training of seminarians and the need for those four pillars to be integrated.[3] This integration is the responsibility of all who are involved in seminary work, not only formators and spiritual directors, but also classroom professors, pastoral supervisors, and all who assist these professionals in their work. In examining the current nature of seminary programs, Sr. Katarina Schuth, OSF, of St. Paul Seminary School of Divinity makes it clear that "all aspects of formation are responsible for the development of virtues related to ministry, such as being compassionate, generous, prudent and consistent in judgments, authentic, and insightful."[4] While this formation of ministerial virtue is a shared responsibility, Schuth is firm in insisting that particular responsibility lies with the directors of human formation (a.k.a. mentors).[5] St. John Paul II also places key importance, however, on the role of the spiritual director because spiritual formation "is the core that unifies and gives life to his being a priest and his acting as a priest" (PDV 45).[6] Therefore, both those who work with seminarians in the external forum and those who work with them in the internal forum need to become alert to the psychological, emotional, developmental, and spiritual currents that are operative within a seminarian.

I have tried to make the case in this book that understanding the nature of archetypal energy is most conducive to an authentic, insightful, and integrated process of formation. It can assist the seminarian (and later priest) with self-knowledge about his desire to live his life nobly for Christ and for the church while being committed to the inner life where he can discover how God stirs within him and how he is better able to make sense of what life experiences are teaching him. Within a comprehension of how archetypal energy operates, a seminarian can discover how to integrate the four pillars of formation. In

---

3. See Katarina Schuth, *Seminary Formation: Recent History, Current Circumstances, New Directions* (Collegeville, MN: Liturgical Press, 2016). She treats the particular connections between human and spiritual formation in chapter 5, pp. 88–99.

4. Ibid., 94.

5. Ibid. In this chapter, I will use the term "mentor" for those who work in the external forum of seminary formation and "spiritual director" for those who work in the internal forum.

6. See also *Program of Priestly Formation*, 5th ed. (Washington, DC: USCCB, 2006), no. 108.

turn, he can learn how to continue to integrate them long after he leaves the safe and supportive structure of initial priestly formation when he will experience his first serious paschal death of what has worked well for him so far spiritually, ministerially, emotionally, and psychologically. Without this awareness of the future narrative of his spiritual journey, a newly ordained priest can fail to correctly discern and successfully navigate what is happening inside of him. Ronald Rolheiser makes this plea:

> Seminary formation must try to develop within its candidates a personal spirituality that is strong enough to sustain the candidate through the ups and downs of a long marathon journey in ministry with its perennial temptations toward inflation or depression. When I think back on my own seminary formation, I see it was strong in teaching me how to do ministry, but it was weak in preparing me *for what ministry would be doing to me*, that is: What would be my temptations to depression, inflation, compensatory actions, manipulation of others, escapism, and anger as I fulfilled my pastoral calling? Seminary formation must strive to develop inside seminarians a personal spirituality that will give them sufficient bread for the long haul. These interior resources are not just for surviving priesthood but for finding joy there and for being a minister of joy to others.[7]

How should seminary formators accomplish this important outcome? Working with the archetypal energies within a future priest's spiritual biography can be very helpful. This boils down to a threefold integrative task: *Welcome the Hero, Train the Servant, and Uncover the Mystic.* In order to understand more fully the specifics of how this could happen in seminary programs, I offer the following fifteen suggestions that arise from the material that has been offered in the previous chapters of this text.

1. Make it clear that priestly spirituality develops in stages. This will mean that mentors and spiritual directors will need to identify and distinguish as clearly as possible for the candidate each of the possible stages within the spiritual biography he is living and will continue to

---

7. Rolheiser, "Toward a Spirituality of Ecclesial Leadership," in Schuth, *Seminary Formation*, 126.

live. Then they ought to explain well the nature of the candidate's current stage of spirituality, most likely within the Noble-Hero-for-Christ archetype, helping him to claim what is wonderful and grace-filled in the present while at the same time preparing him for all the future stages of priestly spirituality that he can expect to enter after ordination. While the seminarian might not retain all of this information, later on when his current archetypal energy unravels, he will remember that he is supposed to be going through this very experience and that it is a good development within his growth as a priest.

2. *Honor the Hero, but know his limits and shadow.* Just because the Hero for Christ is the initial archetype within a priestly biography does not mean it is "merely a phase" a man has to pass through in order to mature. This is the all-important foundation for priestly life and ministry, and the Hero's energy will carry the seminarian/priest through challenges and struggles in all the subsequent stages of priesthood. Most likely, it is Hero energy that has brought a man to the seminary in the first place, and that energy should be welcomed by seminary personnel. Therefore, seminary formators need to help the candidate to recognize, accept, and honor the valiant archetypal energy that has helped him to see the priesthood as a noble vocation and allowed him to take the initial and courageous steps forward. Seminarians should be affirmed for their desire to do great things for Christ and for the church. At the same time, mentors and spiritual directors need to help them see the shadow side of that archetype that lurks within them, that is, the narcissist who craves adulation; the passive-aggressive bully who either gets angry with those who disagree with him or undermines the credibility of perceived opponents; the brooding child who is not getting what he wants; the nasty fault-finder who blames everyone else for what has gone wrong with his plans. Whatever elements of the Hero's shadow are already operative during seminary years need to be addressed by the mentor and spiritual director because that dark energy within an archetype does not simply go away on its own.

3. *Teach seminarians the nature of the False Self and the True Self.* Granted, those candidates who are still in their twenties or early thirties might not yet grasp this distinction experientially, but they soon will. Therefore, the seminary ought to prepare them for it because those who are attentive to the inner life will discover that something more about themselves from deep inside will try to emerge. This is the True Self try-

ing to break through the False Self, which does not mean the False Self was a "Wrong Self" or a "Bad Self," just an earlier sense of one's identity that mostly corresponded to meeting the expectations of others (remember Richard Rohr's definitions in chapter 2). In short, the False Self mostly comes from a response to the outer life. At some point within their spiritual biography, seminarians will discover an identity coming from their inner life, which will eventually move them into the next stage of archetypal energy where they lessen their need to hide their brokenness and win approval through achievement and accomplishment. It is the True Self who will eventually try to break through the seminarians' self-perception; but for younger men who get ordained, this does not often happen until well after they become priests. So they need to be prepared because it will be an unsettling albeit grace-filled experience.

4. *Help a seminarian to "receive his life."* Following St. Ignatius's "Principle and Foundation," a seminarian has to be able to accept genuinely who he is as created by God, but also who he is not. This is the process of "receiving one's life," in which each person is called to recognize with honesty what have been the elements in his biography that he has enjoyed and what have been the painful and difficult elements he has endured. He cannot try to rewrite the biography that has unfolded up to this point in his life, resurfacing one regret after another or grinding his teeth with resentment, all the while avoiding the inner life because of these regrets or resentments. He simply must "receive" it and recognize with gratitude how much God has been with him throughout it all. While not a perfect story, his life has been a graced narrative, as it truly unfolded, without the need for edits, revisions, redactions, or deletions. The capacity to receive his life will prepare the seminarian to do the same with the positive and negative elements of his personal and priestly narrative that will unfold in the future. Furthermore, this foundational capacity will allow the man to recognize where his current archetypal energy has come from, how the Holy Spirit has been operative within that archetype to bring the man to his sense of vocation, and how the Holy Spirit will continue to guide him through the reality of what lies ahead for him. The Spirit who was at work in the reality of a man's past will most assuredly hold him in a future that will not be as ideal as he hopes.

5. *Name the motives.* Spiritual directors and mentors must help seminarians to recognize and admit the underlying, unstated, but very

operative motives within their desire to become a priest. These need not be condemned or immediately discarded, but they need to be brought into the light so that their influence on the man's perception of himself as a priest and the priorities he has for priestly life and ministry can be clearly seen. Also, seminary formators need to prepare candidates to discover that there are other underlying operative motives that they might not become aware of for a long time, but some of those will come to light when they experience the paschal death of the Hero. At the same time, formators need to affirm, strengthen, and deepen the stated and operative motives that truly help seminarians to discover their authentic relationship with Christ and to step into the deeper currents of the spiritual life. These motives may go through their own form of purgation, and seminarians need to know this, but these motives are still to be appreciated as signs of grace-filled cooperation with the Holy Spirit within a man's life. Likewise, knowing how underlying motives can hold sway will prepare seminarians for the times when these motives exert themselves over his emotions, reactions, desires, and interpretation of what he is experiencing in priesthood.

6. *Accept the reality of paschal deaths.* Mentors and spiritual directors have to assist seminarians in their recognition that they "will die a thousand deaths" in their lives and that these are normal experiences, albeit painful. Perhaps formators could share some appropriate examples of the paschal deaths they have experienced thus far in priesthood without overstepping boundaries. This is a crucial lesson for those who are in the Hero archetype stage because the operative energy at this time drives toward success, accomplishment, achievement, and living honorably and well. It does not yet admit to defeat, loss, failure, and the crumbling of the operative motives that have fueled the whole noble venture. The key principle I repeatedly offer seminarians in this regard (which I mentioned in the introduction to this book) is the following: *God will use all of your gifts and abilities in ministry, but God will draw you closer to himself and deeper into yourself through your weakness and inabilities.* Therefore, those in ordained ministry will never be able to avoid paschal deaths; helping seminarians identify the paschal deaths they have already experienced in life (even in small ways) and telling them how priests they respect and admire have gone through such deaths themselves can prepare the gifted and capable Hero for the continuous paschal process that lies ahead.

7. Affirm the Servant instincts in the seminarian. The pastoral formation element of seminary life will do much to reveal the capacity a man has to serve others, how genuine it might be, and how much it still needs to develop. Wherever a seminarian is on the spectrum of servant abilities, the instinct in him that wants to serve God and others ought to be reinforced and prepared for the long haul. Furthermore, a true sense of service needs to be inculcated—one that emerges when there is no reward, no immediately measurable results, no positive feedback. This level of Servant energy is what will help the future priest to stay committed to ministry even when the Hero archetype begins to suffer a paschal death and something deeper needs to come forth. Therefore, mentors and spiritual directors need to probe what a seminarian means when he says he wants to serve God and the church.

8. Instill within seminary candidates the will to communion. Men come to the seminary out of the cauldron of contentiousness that dominates our society. Also, in most cases today, their sense of vocation will emerge from an experience of religious awakening and commitment that wants clarity, distinctiveness, and boldness. While this is certainly wonderful heroic energy, it also lends itself to intolerance, black-and-white thinking, and dismissiveness toward those whose view of religion differs (whether they are members of the Catholic Church, people of other denominations of religions, or those who do not practice religion at all). Therefore, they will have to be cautioned about this, even challenged at times. Furthermore, they ought to be led to a discovery of whatever psychological and emotional needs lie underneath their religious energy that seeks clarity, distinctiveness, and boldness. This can prevent their religious energy from becoming a mask for what really ought to be attended to in a man's growth and development. In addition, in order for a will to communion to emerge, seminarians will have to be taught how this comes from the very nature of the Trinity, the priestly heart of Christ, and the desire of the church for a priest to be a man of communion. Without a true will to communion the seminarian's impending *promise of obedience* will be very provisional without his realizing it. While he may truly like his bishop at the moment, his bishop has probably not yet asked of him something very difficult. Or while he may feel a kindred spirit with his current bishop, the same may not be true of his successors, to whom he also promises obedience. The will to communion is the important capacity to see beyond the differences on the surface and discover a deeper oneness that supersedes them and to "will" out of that deeper oneness. Finally, mentors and spiritual directors will need to lead seminarians to the most sustainable source for a will to communion, which comes from the recognition of one's own brokenness and that all persons are broken. As chapter 3 described, in our communion with Christ in our own brokenness do we find communion with all others in theirs.

9. Teach seminarians how to contemplate and discern in their prayer. Seminaries are obligated to instruct seminarians how to recite the Divine Office, participate correctly and well in the Liturgy of the Eucharist, and lead the rosary and other key devotional prayers that are important to God's People, and rightly so. All of these forms of vital public and communal prayers will not, however, always be enough to help future priests navigate the turbulent waters of the paschal process as they are led through the difficult shifts from one archetype to another. This is why personal prayer has to be modeled and encouraged by seminary formators. Do not assume seminarians will learn deep personal prayer or how to discern all by themselves or just because they have been apprised of their importance. Seminarians need to be mentored in the practice of *lectio divina*, Ignatian prayer, discernment of spirits, centering prayer, etc. If they are not introduced to these practices while in the seminary, they may never discover how to engage in them effectively later.

10. Help extroverts to go inward toward Christ. Extroverts have to discover the reality of the inner life and to recognize it as a true meeting place with Christ. They need to know that they will not survive in priesthood merely by engaging energetically and constantly in the outer life of ministry. Formators should help extroverts adopt strategies of being able to spend greater lengths of time alone in quiet solitude and prayer. Even extroverts can be led to discover the nature of the Mystic who dwells deep inside of them.

11. Help introverts to let Christ into their deep interior. Up until now in their lives, most seminarians who are introverts have experienced their inner lives as a place of refuge, of welcome respite from having to spend so much energy being with others. While this is a strong basis for a deeper prayer life, many introverts have not learned how to let Christ be with them in their inner sanctuary. Many introverts ruminate inside their heads without letting Christ into their inner monologue. Formators ought not to assume that a quiet person is a prayerful person or that someone who is comfortable being alone has definitely learned the spirituality of solitude. Spiritual directors especially ought to ask introverted seminarians the content of their inner lives in order to discover how best to mentor them in prayerful solitude that includes the company of Christ and his Spirit. Even introverts need to find out how to be yoked to Christ in their quiet pondering.

12. Introduce seminarians to silent, directed retreats. By the end of their first year in theology, after they have had enough familiarity with group, preached retreats, make sure that seminarians have a good experience of a silent, directed retreat. They need to value their yearly retreat as a unique opportunity to encounter Christ and themselves in their deepest deep. Without meaningful, sustained contact with the underlying currents of the spiritual life, any seminarian or priest will remain stuck in archetypal energy he should have long outgrown. As an additional benefit, the intensified practice of prayer while on a silent, directed retreat could find its way into the daily life of the seminarian and priest. This will assist them in later recognizing and responding to the call of their inner Mystic.

13. Do not stay focused only on observable behavior or self-reporting by the seminarian. It is imperative that eventually in a spiritual direction relationship, after a good level of trust has been built, directors need to do more than discuss only what seminarians present for discussion and begin to probe with them what is stirring inside of them. If all spiritual direction does is to help seminarians avoid the dark and murky waters inside of them by talking around them or not even naming them out loud to a trusted spiritual guide, then it actually contributes to future patterns of denial, avoidance, or misdirection. These patterns prevent those things that really need to be examined from being brought into the light and then into prayer. The Hero does not yet want to deal with all of his brokenness and, in a certain sense, is not able to. That is fine, but in order to prevent the shadow side of the Hero from taking over, the dark and murky stuff inside a seminarian will have to be discussed at some point so it can be integrated in a more healthy manner.

14. Celibacy must be talked about candidly. The commitment to celibacy cannot be overspiritualized or merely contained within a pious approach to priesthood, as expressed in sentiments like "God is all I need" by someone who still barely knows God and certainly does not yet fully know the needs of the "I" uttering those words.

Furthermore, celibacy cannot be de-sexualized by only discussing it in terms of utility (i.e., "It will make you more available in ministry") or as a substitutionary virtue (i.e., "While you will not have your own family, you will become a member of many families"). While there is truth in both of these claims and they certainly do appeal to the Hero-for-Christ and the Servant-with-Christ archetypes, by themselves these notions will not carry the man through present and future nights of loneliness and longing. They will not appease the inherent need for intimacy that lies at the core of every human being's sexuality. Therefore, celibacy must be discussed as a wonderful and fulfilling expression of the man's sexual self, though it will be quite different from how he may have expressed his sexual energy in the past before a serious commitment to Christ emerged in his life. Ultimately the generativity that beckons underneath the seminarian's heroic, self-giving interpretations of celibacy has to lead him to his inner Mystic's communion with Christ deep inside of him.

15. Celebrate and teach the Eucharist well. Help seminarians to learn theologically and experience fruitfully that the Eucharist is a multilayered reality that will come to mean different things to them at different points in their ministry. The more they can comprehend theologically the different layers of this core sacrament, the more all that Christ's real presence in the Eucharist can offer to them will come to fruition and, through them, be of benefit to others. Challenge them not to interpret or speak about the Eucharist only in one way, since it has so many different elements of understanding. Among them are the following: a celebration of the Real Presence of Christ, a Mass of sacrifice and praise, a pivotal act of worship that expresses thanksgiving to God, a sacred meal that is shared with others, the "missioning" of the Body of Christ out into the world, the intimate experience of communion with Christ and with each other, etc. Since the archetypal narrative within a priest's spiritual life is a multilayered reality, then a priest needs to appreciate all the layers of the Eucharist in order for each priestly archetypal energy within him to be nourished and sustained. In this way the Eucharist will remain a constant center of his priestly life and ministry as he navigates the shifting currents of his archetypal energy. Furthermore, the more the Eucharist is allowed to be all that it can be for a priest, then the more it will beckon him to go deeper into his spiritual life.

Part 2: The Archetypes in Ongoing Priestly Formation

Support the Hero; Strengthen the Servant; Evoke the Mystic

Recall the words of St. John Paul II from *Pastores Dabo Vobis* cited in the introduction of this book: "Every life is a constant path toward maturity, a maturity which cannot be attained except by constant formation" (PDV 70). He further goes on to say rather emphatically:

> In this sense, the entire particular church has the responsibility, under the guidance of the bishop, to develop and look after the different aspects of her priests' permanent formation. Priests are not there to serve themselves but the People of God. So, ongoing formation, in ensuring the human, spiritual, intellectual and pastoral maturity of priests, is doing good to the People of God itself. (PDV 78)

Yet somehow during seminary years, "formation" became a reviled term for future priests that often retains that connotation long after ordination, unless a priest is talking about what *another* guy might need (one of those "Difficult Other Priests"). Cast in the negative light of feeling constantly watched as a seminarian by the faculty, most often priests will later instinctively react negatively to all discussion about the need for ongoing formation. That reaction often becomes dismissiveness toward any prescribed days of recollection, continuing education opportunities, or priest convocations or symposia.

The term "ongoing formation" is, however, really a more clinical word for "ongoing conversion" that every Christian man and woman undergoes if one truly stays attentive to the spiritual life. Why should priests be exempt from such a process? Even the US bishops, in response to the clarion call by Pope John Paul II for the ongoing formation of priests, issued a *ratio fundamentalis* (a charter document) for diocesan programs to implement ongoing formation. Titled *The Basic Plan for the Ongoing Formation of Priests*, the US bishops remarkably began their plan with the following pledge:

> In obedient response to the Holy Father's express wishes, we commit ourselves to supplying the necessary personnel, time, and finances to make the ongoing formation of priests an effective reality in the life of our dioceses. We will do our best in our respective dioceses. We will also join forces regionally and

nationally, when that kind of collective and collaborative effort
and investment will better serve the purpose of ongoing formation for priests.

We commit ourselves to reminding our priests of the importance of ongoing formation. We will encourage them in their
efforts, and we will call them to accountability in the name of the
Church. Furthermore, we will support our priests by informing
the entire people of God that the prayer and study of their priests
is not something added on to their work but rather is integral to
their ministry.

Finally, we commit ourselves to participating in the process of
ongoing formation. The Holy Father has said, "The Bishop will
live up to his responsibility, not only by seeing to it that his presbyterate has places and times for its ongoing formation, but also
by being present in person and taking part in an interested and
friendly way" (PDV, no. 79).[8]

This pledge from the bishops in 2001 cannot be allowed to fade from
their memories or be demoted within their list of priorities. It was
made only one year before the terrible eruption of the clergy abuse
scandal across the country and the bishops' subsequent response to
that scandal in the form of the Dallas Charter. Since that painful moment, this previous pledge by the bishops ought to be repeated and
reaffirmed with even greater zeal. It is imperative that priests be held
accountable to ongoing development as human beings, spiritual persons, intellectual teachers on behalf of the church, and pastoral ministers. No longer can the church assume this will happen on its own,
since it does not happen this way with any group of persons. The
bishops need to model this commitment to ongoing formation themselves and then, with authenticity, challenge their priests to make the
same commitment. As their pledge makes clear, bishops are not only
to oversee a program of ongoing formation of priests but also to participate in it themselves "in an interested and friendly way."

---

8. United States Conference of Catholic Bishops, *The Basic Plan for the Ongoing Formation of Priests* (2001), introduction. http://www.usccb.org/beliefs-and-
teachings/vocations/priesthood/priestly-life-and-ministry/national-plan-for-the
-ongoing-formation-of-priests.cfm.

The US bishops recognize that the key to ongoing priestly formation is integration, as it is with initial formation programs in seminaries. The bishops define integration in the following manner:

> For many, the word "integration" may be either vague or seem to reduce spirituality to psychological processes. In the context of ongoing formation, integration is quite specific and spiritual. It signals the movement toward a unity of life that draws together and dynamically relates who we are, what we do, and what we are about (our purpose or mission). As a movement toward a unity of life, the aim of integration is to find the *unum necessarium*, "the one necessary thing," of the Gospel and to live centered in it.[9]

That "one necessary thing" the bishops recognize to be the true centering principle of priestly life and ministry in all of its stages is union with Christ, who calls us at the beginning of our vocations and throughout them to put out into the deep water. If the ongoing response by priests to that call of Christ is to be truly integrative, then it must involve all the archetypal energies that shape and energize priests along the way. Within a comprehensive approach to ongoing formation for priests there must be attention given to what the Hero will struggle with, what the Servant needs in order to keep going, and what the Mystic is being led to discover and then offer to the church. Similar to initial priestly formation, this means a threefold integrative task: *Support the Hero, Strengthen the Servant, Evoke the Mystic.* Although this task parallels that of seminary formation, there are some key differences.

The first set of differences comes from within a priest. Primarily, ongoing formation does not deal with men who are as "formable" as younger candidates for priesthood. Second, mistaken interpretations of the theological concept of the "ontological change" in priests make some men conclude they are finished products after ordination and

---

9. Ibid., part 1, section C. The entire plan by the US bishops is well worth the read. It is quite detailed about both dimensions of ongoing formation, what the bishops call the "synchronic" dimensions that apply all throughout priesthood and the "diachronic" dimensions specific to each stage within it. Because of its detail, I will not be repeating their valuable and comprehensive plan but will instead suggest some guiding principles based on the template of priestly life offered in this book.

no longer in need of formation. (NB: No seminary that I am aware of is teaching this, but that has not completely eradicated the misconception.) Third, resistance to being challenged increases when a man's comfortable world is coming apart, as will happen with each paschal death. That resistance can be met head-on in seminary formation, but nothing necessarily engages that resistance after ordination. A fourth difference is evidenced by priests in crisis. It is no secret that such priests often stop praying, and many never take the rightful steps to seek help. In the seminary, a mentor or spiritual director could offer challenge, support, and assistance. No one systematically does that for priests in crisis.

The second set of differences arises from the nature of priestly life and ministry as opposed to seminary life. First among these is that there are not effective structures of accountability, as the ones that were operative in the seminary, that can now hold priests to the demands of ongoing formation. Who asks a priest if he is meeting regularly with a spiritual director? What happens if a priest does not come to days of recollection or does not make his annual retreat? Who challenges a priest who is developing unhealthy patterns in his personal life? Second, the work load and stress level for many priests can be so great that they simply do not find the time or have the energy to participate in opportunities for ongoing formation, even if they fundamentally support them. Unlike in seminaries, no one generally challenges them if they do not show up. A third difference is that the ideological divide among priests (as described in the previous chapter) makes it difficult to find speakers, retreat leaders, and facilitators that are acceptable to the presbyterate as a whole. While this is also true among seminarians, they are still obligated to attend seminary functions no matter what. A fourth distinction is that seminarians get a decent amount of time off, but sabbaticals are shrinking among priests. With the decreasing number of priests in many dioceses, the encouragement to go on sabbatical is also decreasing and perhaps with it also the opportunities to go on sabbatical. A fifth difference is this: unlike seminary personnel who are guided by the *PPF* and who implement it as a collective body, sometimes those who are responsible for overseeing the ongoing formation of priests in their diocese are doing it all by themselves and in many ways simply do not know what it all entails or how best to go about it. Often they keep in place what has already been established, regardless of whether it is effective. Finally, while seminaries put into their schedules the opportunities for mentoring and spiritual direction, as well as other mandated experiences of formation in all four pillars, hardworking priests sometimes feel that formation opportunities are an interruption to what they should be doing. Sometimes they also have to deal with parishioners who make dismissive comments about the priest "taking *another* day off" for a conference or "getting *another* vacation" when a priest is actually going on retreat. This attitude, which suggests that ongoing formation opportunities are taking men away from what they ought to be doing, needs to be exorcised from priests and the church as a whole.

If ongoing priestly formation is ever going to gain ground within dioceses, then bishops and their presbyterates have to value it and then insist on an effective manner of providing it. This could be the role of the Servants with Christ among the presbyterate who have discovered the fruitfulness of a different level of personal prayer that has kept them going after their first major paschal death of the Hero for Christ and all the other paschal deaths along the way. They need to step forward and contribute to ways to walk with their brother priests along the same path that Christ has been walking with them. Likewise, the Mystics in Christ within the presbyterate ought to challenge their brothers to find ways to go deeper into themselves so that they too can be drawn into the powerful place of communion with Christ within their own brokenness from which they can no longer hide. The influence of these two groups of priests could bring the whole presbyterate to a place of recognition that ongoing formation is essential. Once priests get to that place, the following are some suggested principles about how best to draw into ongoing formation (or ongoing conversion) all three major archetypes of priesthood within the presbyterate. To put it another way, here are some recommendations for building a local church's ark-of-types by supporting the Hero, strengthening the Servant, and evoking the Mystic.

1. Bishops need to help to build and then steer the ark-of-types that is within their own presbyterate. No efforts at ongoing formation of priests will happen without a bishop's energetic support. Any plans for ongoing formation ought not to arise merely out of a reactive mode to the personnel problems with which a bishop has had to deal. Instead, these plans ought to arise out of a vision of the healthy developmental journey that needs to occur within all priests—a journey that includes attentiveness to the four pillars of formation and that recognizes how different archetypal energies are at work within the same presbyterate.

2. Find the right mentor-pastors for the newly ordained. The first months and years after ordination are critical; they are a mixture of great joy and enthusiasm over the opportunities in priestly ministry and also the anguish of paschal deaths when one's noble ideas meet head-on the hardened realities of ministry. Therefore, those responsible for clergy assignments ought to make sure that pastors of newly ordained men can welcome the heroes and direct with wisdom the zeal and conviction they bring without stifling them, belittling them, or suggesting they just need to get beyond their idealism. These pastors should be well-schooled in how Hero archetypal energy works and how it is a great gift to the church. They also need to be made aware of the Hero's shadow side and how best to meet it and challenge it with fraternal care and not belligerent or condescending anger.

3. Gather the newly ordained regularly for prayer, fellowship, and input. Many newly ordained priests enjoyed the day-to-day support of their peers while they were in the seminary. The sudden loss of that kind of contact can be very unsettling, especially if now they are living with only one other priest who might be considerably older than them. In some dioceses, newly ordained priests are living by themselves only one or two years after they have left the seminary. Therefore, gathering the newly ordained together regularly allows them to experience peer support once again and to affirm each other's honorable efforts in ministry. It also allows them to hear each other's disappointments and struggles in a more accepting manner and to offer each other support and encouragement. At the same time, however, the continuance of their human, intellectual, spiritual, and pastoral formation needs to occur. The right mentor (or mentors) of this valuable group of men could provide sessions that strengthen their valiant energy but also help them navigate the paschal deaths already occurring within their Hero archetype.

4. Do not expect the Hero to work out his anger or disappointment on his own. Assigning the right mentor to a newly ordained man is crucial. The mentor needs to understand the stages within a priest's spiritual journey and how the onset of anger and disappointment, along with frustration and loneliness, is part of the paschal process that every good priest must undergo over and over again. Therefore, what the newly ordained priest is experiencing needs to be recognized, respected, and then remedied through deeper forms of prayer and more honest levels of insight into oneself.

5. *Do not let a Hero endure a paschal death alone and without honor.* His paschal death *will* occur if the priest remains attentive to his spiritual life. Therefore, a mentor needs to accompany him through the paschal process, reassuring him of a new Pentecost at the end of it all. It would be good if this mentor could share appropriately some of the paschal deaths he himself has experienced and how a deeper commitment to prayer surfaced within him a deeper level of archetypal energy and a deeper spirit of priesthood that rose from the paschal death of his heroic energy.

6. *Make spiritual directors easily available to priests and then strongly urge them to participate regularly in spiritual direction.* It is alarming how many priests who are charged with the care of souls are not being mentored in the care of their own soul. The most important dimension of their priestly identity is their inner life, which is not automatically nourished and sustained by the responsibilities of ministry or the commitment to praying the Office. No matter which archetypal energy a priest exhibits, to have a trustworthy objective voice within one's spiritual journey is so important to continued growth in one's spiritual biography and in one's ability to put out into even deeper waters than before.

7. *Include within days of recollection the learning of different forms of personal prayer.* As with seminarians so with priests: it cannot be assumed that they will learn on their own how to develop a deeper prayer life. That important formative piece needs to be taught, modeled, and then taught some more and modeled again.

8. *Encourage priest faith-sharing groups.* So many priests who participate in support groups like those of the Emmaus Program or Jesus Caritas attest over and over again to the tremendous benefit their group has brought to their priestly life and ministry. To be most effective for establishing true communion within the presbyterate, it would be best if the groups could include all the different stages of priestly development so that all the different archetypes are at the table of discussion and prayer with each other, offering to each other what they uniquely bring to the table.

9. Gather larger groups of priests together in a more purposeful manner. While it can be difficult to find the right *speaker* for priest days of recollection or continuing education opportunities, it might be more productive to find the right *facilitator* who will offer some input to the priests but then capably evoke from them at tables of discussion their own insights, experiences, hopes, ideas, and worries. It is imperative that priests assist each other in ongoing formation and not only rely on some "expert" to do it for them. Within a local presbyterate there is a tremendous collective wisdom that needs to be tapped into and disclosed in gatherings that are effectively designed to do that. This is why the right facilitator is important. It is also important that more and more opportunities be provided for priests to be at table with each other—tables of discussion, support, respect, and even a certain appropriate level of self-disclosure. So often at these tables, certain negative conclusions that one priest might have about another are recognized as misconceptions and a new level of desire for communion can unfold.

10. Strengthen the Servant's capacity to serve in ever newer and deeper ways. The majority of a man's years as a priest will probably be shaped by the Faithful Servant-with-Christ archetypal energy. In that long stretch of time, however, the needs of the church will constantly shift, as will his own place of ministry. Therefore, the Servant priest's spiritual companionship with Christ needs to be affirmed, nourished, and strengthened by days of recollection and opportunities for spiritual direction. In addition, his current skills as a Servant will need to be honed as he faces the ever-increasing complexity of the needs of God's People; he will also need to learn new skills to meet new challenges. Therefore, encourage, support, and affirm the Servant who will minister in his own particular way in each particular assignment. Then stretch his horizon and teach him whatever particular abilities are needed for each new Pentecost moment within the local church and the priest's own life. This includes the skills and knowledge to be a new pastor, a teacher in specialized ministry, a member of diocesan administration, a chaplain in a hospital or prison, or a priest who is now a senior associate or a retired priest. Again, do not assume a priest will pick up by himself the skills he needs for any new moment in ministry or know how to better the skills he already has.

11. Do not let a Servant endure a paschal death alone or without being thanked. Support and encourage him as he begins the difficult paschal death that is leading deeper into his broken self and into the deepest waters in his inner life. This "second fathom of desolation" (as described in chapter 3) might manifest itself in the priest's listlessness about ministry, his increasing absence from priest gatherings, or his noticeable silence when he is present. Or he might be more irritable and irascible than normal. This is when the one who is responsible for ongoing formation needs to make sure the priest knows how much his ministry all these years has been appreciated. Furthermore, the director of ongoing formation should make sure that this priest has a spiritual director who can understand what he is going through. In some way this man ought to be connected with a priest who evidences the Mystic-in-Christ stage of spiritual development. The Mystic's ability to receive with graciousness what the "dying" Servant is experiencing will make all the difference. He can remind the Servant how valuable all his years of service have been and also offer advice about how to engage prayerfully and valiantly this new level of paschal death, especially as it involves embracing his own wounds and fractured personal narrative.

   12. Identify the Mystics who could become skilled spiritual directors. The previous principle and all the others before it would work better if within each presbyterate there were some devoted priests evidencing the archetypal energy of the Mystic in Christ who have been trained in spiritual direction. At the very least, these men should be identified and then supported in seeking the appropriate training to become qualified, skilled spiritual directors, especially to other priests. Such candidates are there, within each presbyterate; however, they have to be identified, trained, and supported. Again, a presbyterate should not assume these individuals will surface by themselves and find the training they need on their own.

   13. Promote silent, directed retreats. Priests can keep the Mystic within them at bay for a while in priesthood, but the very nature of their ministry, their celibacy, and their eucharistic identity will keep calling them to embrace the Mystic archetypal energy inside of them. To completely ignore it well into the second half of their lives will cause them to become pathologically stuck in patterns of compensatory behavior, underdeveloped maturity, or shallow coping mechanisms. Only meaningful and significant encounters with silence will allow the Mystic in Christ to emerge. Therefore, those responsible for coordinating priest retreats ought to encourage men to go on a silent, directed retreat, if not yearly then at least every other year. Our deeper inner life demands silence, and a correct interpretation of what arises from our deeper self needs an objective director to assist. The merits of such a retreat were outlined in chapter 1 as the second imperative for priests undergoing the regular difficulties and disappointments of ministry. A further benefit of encouraging silent, directed retreats, however, is that the one who has to coordinate priest retreats will not need to worry about a presenter who is acceptable to everyone.

14. Give room for mysticism within the apostolic life. Even diocesan priests are called to tap into the Mystic that beckons from within. It is where Christ is leading all who believe in him. In his book *Quickening the Fire in Our Midst: The Challenge of Diocesan Priestly Spirituality*, George Aschenbrenner, a Jesuit quite familiar with an apostolic life of priesthood, challenges all who live the nonmonastic life to discover their genuine "monasticism of the heart."[10] In that text, Aschenbrenner insists that this is a necessary foundation for the active life of the diocesan priest. He describes it as something that "anchors the Christian identity in an experience of God that is far beyond anything of this world . . . , one that strips and purifies, scouring the heart to a radical solitude in and with God."[11] Directors of ongoing formation programs need to introduce priests to this concept and make it acceptable for them to explore it more fully. This includes making it a part of the "ministerial contracts" for priests that, besides a weekly day off, they also ought to be afforded at least one day a month for quiet solitude and prayer.

15. Encourage priests to pray with each other and for each other. Every presbyterate names their bishop in every recitation of a eucharistic prayer, and rightly so. But within their praying of the Office and their own personal prayer, priests need to bring into their communion with Christ their care and concern for each other. As described in chapter 4, our own deeper communion with Christ cannot be truly authentic if it does not include communion with each other, including

---

10. George Aschenbrenner, *Quickening the Fire in Our Midst: The Challenge of Diocesan Priestly Spirituality* (Chicago: Loyola Press, 2002). See chapter 3, "God's Love: Alone and Enough," 16–26.

11. Ibid., 17.

the "Difficult Others" in our lives. The more priests can be conscious of the others in their presbyterate during their prayer, the more they will seek out ways to be at table with each other, to call out what is best in each other, and to offer each other whatever assistance, wisdom, challenge, and insight they can. And they will offer it out of a sense of respect and brotherhood. This is one of the most fruitful practices within the ongoing formation for priests that could ever evolve within a presbyterate.

The River Always Beckons

Then the angel showed me the river of the water of life, bright as crystal, flowing from the throne of God and of the Lamb.
—Revelation 22:1

It has been many years since I last attempted to navigate the sometimes vexing waters of the Clarion River, but the experience has become embedded in me. Only now the river has become the flowing stream of the spiritual life that not only keeps trying to lead me to Christ but flows out of Christ into me, into each and every one of us. St. John's vision in the book of Revelation of the "water of life . . . flowing from the throne of God and of the Lamb" actually captures the desire of God to draw each one of us into the spiritual waters that carry us to his side and to a place of incredible intimacy with his Son. And so the river keeps calling us, over and over again. In my own spiritual biography, there have been times that the river has been calm with the water's current flowing smoothly. At other moments it has been very turbulent and fraught with things that can get me stuck in the muck and mire of life or the mess of my own broken self. Still other times it can seem to be shallow and drying up, giving rise to a frustration within me that wants to just get out of the river altogether. Yet, wonderful spiritual mentors throughout my life and priests I have met who have truly become Mystics in Christ have constantly inspired me to stay in the river and find the deeper stream.

In addition, just as I had to learn that a kayak was a better vessel than a canoe for navigating the Clarion River (at least in the late summer), in my spiritual biography I have needed to discover how to traverse the deeper waters not in a vessel of solitary effort and endurance but in an ark of communion. As chapter 4 made clear, the right vessel for the successful navigation of the flowing waters of the spiritual life is an ark of communion with all the different layers of who I truly am. I could not leave any part of myself out of the boat—not anything in my past, nothing of my present life, and none of the things that stir inside of me. All of this was being drawn into the stream of God's love, and I needed to surrender it into the current, one small particle after another and then another, and so on. Furthermore, it has been important for me to recognize that this vessel of priestly spirituality is also an ark of communion with all the different priests who are a part of my own priestly life and ministry and all the different ways that they live priesthood, not only those who have greatly inspired me and assisted me over the years, but also those who live a manner of priesthood that is very different from mine. Most important, however, I needed to learn how to enter and stay within the ark of communion with Christ who lives in my deepest core, underneath what is wounded and broken within me, summoning me to find there his intimate presence that I would not be able to discover in any other place or in any other way. Christ has constantly called me to enter deep inside of myself where he dwells so that he could take me deeper into himself where I am called to dwell. This invitation of Christ has revealed to me the real meaning of St. Paul's words, "It is no longer I who live, but it is Christ who lives in me" (Gal 2:20). Clearly Christ's invitation is not meant only for me but is a summons for everyone who believes in him and desires to go deeper into the spiritual life.

As I stated at the outset of this book, my own boyhood struggles with the Clarion River have become a paradigmatic experience of what would later be my struggles in the spiritual life. At the same time, learning the secret of the Clarion River—finding the deeper stream—has also been paradigmatic for me. It has been symbolic of what I have come to realize I am always called to do in my spiritual biography as a priest. I wish I could say that whenever I have been able to enter that deeper stream that I always ended up experiencing joy, fulfillment, and inner peace, but this has simply not been the case all the time. It took me years before I could embrace the sacred necessity of the paschal process in myself that has needed to unfold over and over again. It is amazing that we priests are often so good at preaching about the paschal mystery but can seem as resistant as anyone else to embracing it in our own lives. We can be just as unwilling as others to let the paschal mystery take hold of us in order to transform us more fully into Christ by bringing us into a deeper fathom of the waters of the spiritual life. I am as guilty as anyone when it comes to this. But now I have come to a place of self-honesty that admits how I would never have endured in priesthood or grown in the spiritual life had it not been for the very difficult paschal moments in my life.

At times students will ask me about who were the greatest teachers I had. Immediately I always think of some of the most wonderful instructors who taught me as I was growing up and some of the most insightful professors who taught me in seminary and while doing doctoral studies. If the students who pose the question to me are ready for a real honest answer, however, I reply, "Painful experiences." The painful elements of the paschal process that have arisen so often in my own spiritual biography have taught me how to go deeper into the spiritual life because it has become so clear that nothing else would transform those experiences of pain into encounters with grace. I am not advocating a masochistic spirituality that values only the wounds and woes of life. Instead, it is my observation that the more people skirt around discovering the meaning of the painful moments of their lives and the wounded dimensions of themselves then the less they enter the depths of the spiritual life.

Therefore, I plead with all you priests and seminarians who are experiencing any level of anguish or heartache, please find the right person to lead you through the paschal grace that can come from it. In addition, connect with other seminarians and priests from whom you can find support and encouragement because of their own familiarity with the same experience. If you are struggling to feel in your gut what it means to be loved by God, then talk about it with a spiritual director and discover how to rightfully bring that struggle into your prayer. In this way God can reveal how much he has been with you throughout the sometimes fulfilling and sometimes fractured narrative of your life so far. I have discovered in spiritual direction sessions with seminarians and priests over the years that as surely as they have felt called by God, so many have not yet felt with any certainty being loved by him. Only the paschal process can lead to that experience, when the crying out for God in our distress opens us up to receive what God has always desired to be for us and now we are finally letting him be.

Furthermore, if you are now at a place in your ministry where you are realizing that your Hero archetype is entering a paschal death, bring it to a spiritual director who can help you claim the blessings of what that energy has been in your vocational journey but also help you to recognize that a different archetypal energy is now trying to emerge from within you. While this may be the end of the Hero stage of your commitment to God and the church, it does not mean that your vocation is over or that it was never genuine in the first place. It simply means that you are moving further along in the lifelong conversion process of "coming to full stature in Christ."

I offer the same counsel to the priests who have prayed with Christ at their side for many years and have ministered in Christ's name with great fidelity for so long but who are now experiencing a paschal death of their Servant archetype. The satisfaction and fulfillment found in years of faithful service may be coming apart. This does not mean all those years were wasted. Instead it signals that henceforth the deeper journey inward can happen more fully. The Mystic within is calling out to you, from the center of your broken self that you may have avoided embracing all these years.

Therefore, I encourage every priest to find the deeper stream of priestly spirituality and then keep putting out into those deeper waters. In this way, Christ can ontologically claim every part of who we are as human beings and priests—all that we have been made to be by God and all that we are experientially, developmentally, emotionally and psychologically, sexually, spiritually, and sacramentally—in our brokenness and in our fulfillment. Christ's ontological claim on us as both human beings and priests allows whatever painful paschal processes that unfold to become transforming encounters with grace and new Pentecosts of deeper conversion.

It is my hope that this book may help seminarians and priests who have said yes to Christ's call to priesthood to recognize in that yes an assent not only to do heroic things for Christ and to serve faithfully with Christ but also heroically and faithfully to enter the flowing waters of the spiritual life. Furthermore, may their yes give voice to the pull of the Mystic in Christ inside of them to stay within those waters no matter how turbulent they become, to go deeper into them, and to draw life from them.

The importance of vibrant inner lives for priests cannot be understated. So often today people will remark, "Our world needs heroes." Well, so does our church. Likewise, our church needs amazingly selfless ministers and profoundly wise spiritual guides who, along with those heroes, will lead others to Christ. The ark-of-types that is priesthood provides the Heroes, the Servants, and the Mystics that God's People deeply desire and need. May all the men who are preparing to enter that ark or who already dwell within it truly be for God's People everything that God has called them to be. Moreover, the archetypal energy of good and holy priests can encourage other men and women to become Noble Heroes for Christ, Faithful Servants with Christ, and Humble Mystics in Christ who is in them. For this to happen more effectively, the church needs priests who look for the deeper spiritual waters within themselves. Therefore, the "river of the water of life," which St. John envisages "flowing from the throne of God and of the Lamb," is not only a revelation of our eternal destiny; it is also a vision of what takes place now in our spiritual biography. That river always beckons.